CRITICAL THINKING IN CLINICAL PRACTICE IN SPEECH-LANGUAGE PATHOLOGY

Cheryl D. Gunter and Joseph B. LeJeune

Cover image © Shutterstock, Inc.

www.kendallhunt.com
Send all inquiries to:
4050 Westmark Drive
Dubuque, IA 52004-1840

ISBN 978-1-5249-8556-1

Published in the United States of America

DEDICATION

We dedicate this work to those whom we have been honored to serve as clinical educators and clinical practitioners.

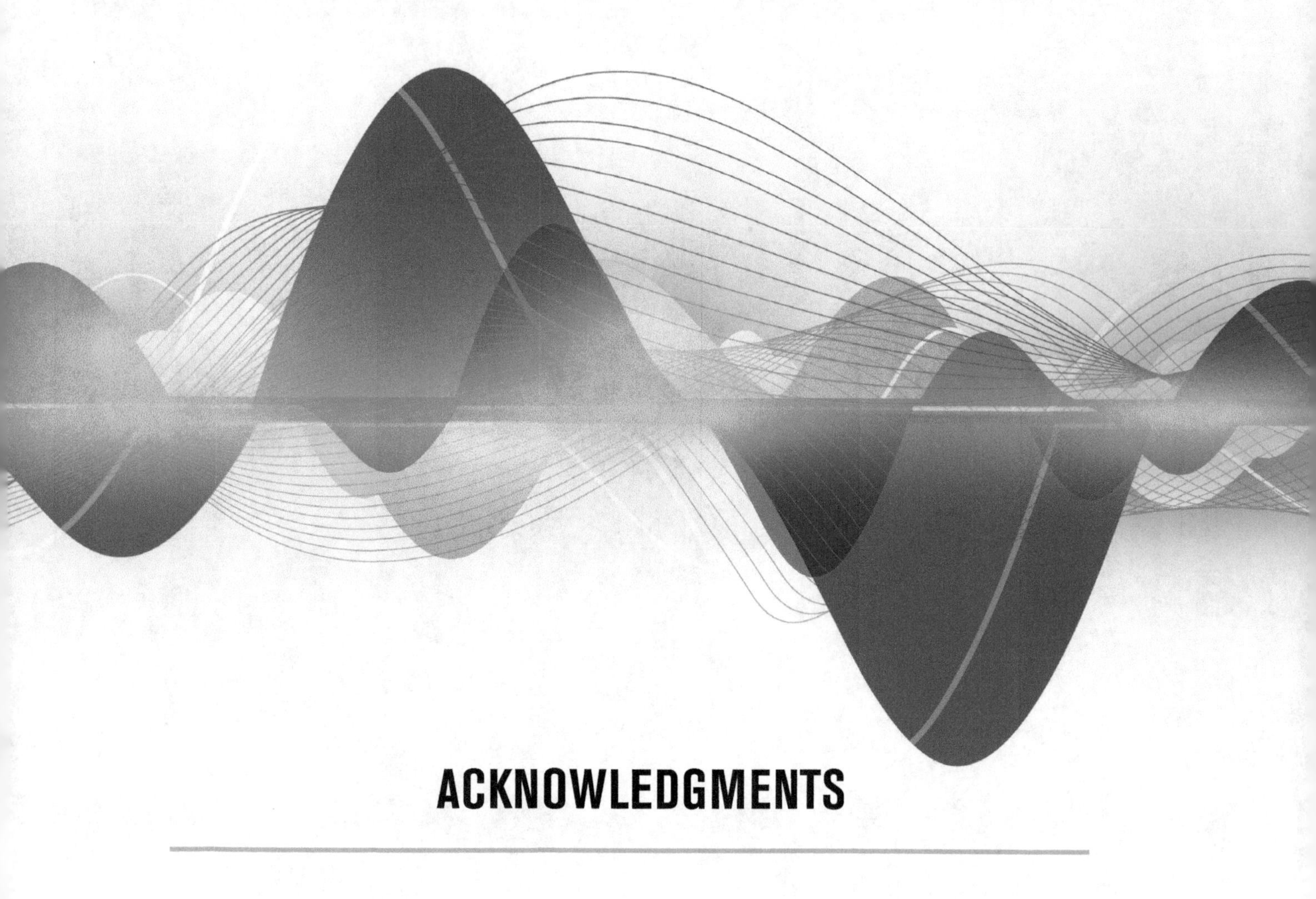

ACKNOWLEDGMENTS

We wish to express our sincere appreciation for the positive and perpetual support provided to us by two extraordinarily special people, Paul A. Rabe and Joseph R. LeJeune.

We also wish to express our sincere appreciation to the West Chester University College of Health Sciences for the financial support for our research in the form of a WCU CHS Teacher-Scholar Grant.

We wish to express our sincere appreciation to the staff of Kendall-Hunt Publishers, particularly Ryan L. Schrodt and his immensely talented production team.

We also wish to express our sincere appreciation to those who choose to incorporate this book into their instruction, supervision, and administration to enhance their own professional development, as well as to promote the enhancement of the clinical competence of those whom they mentor.

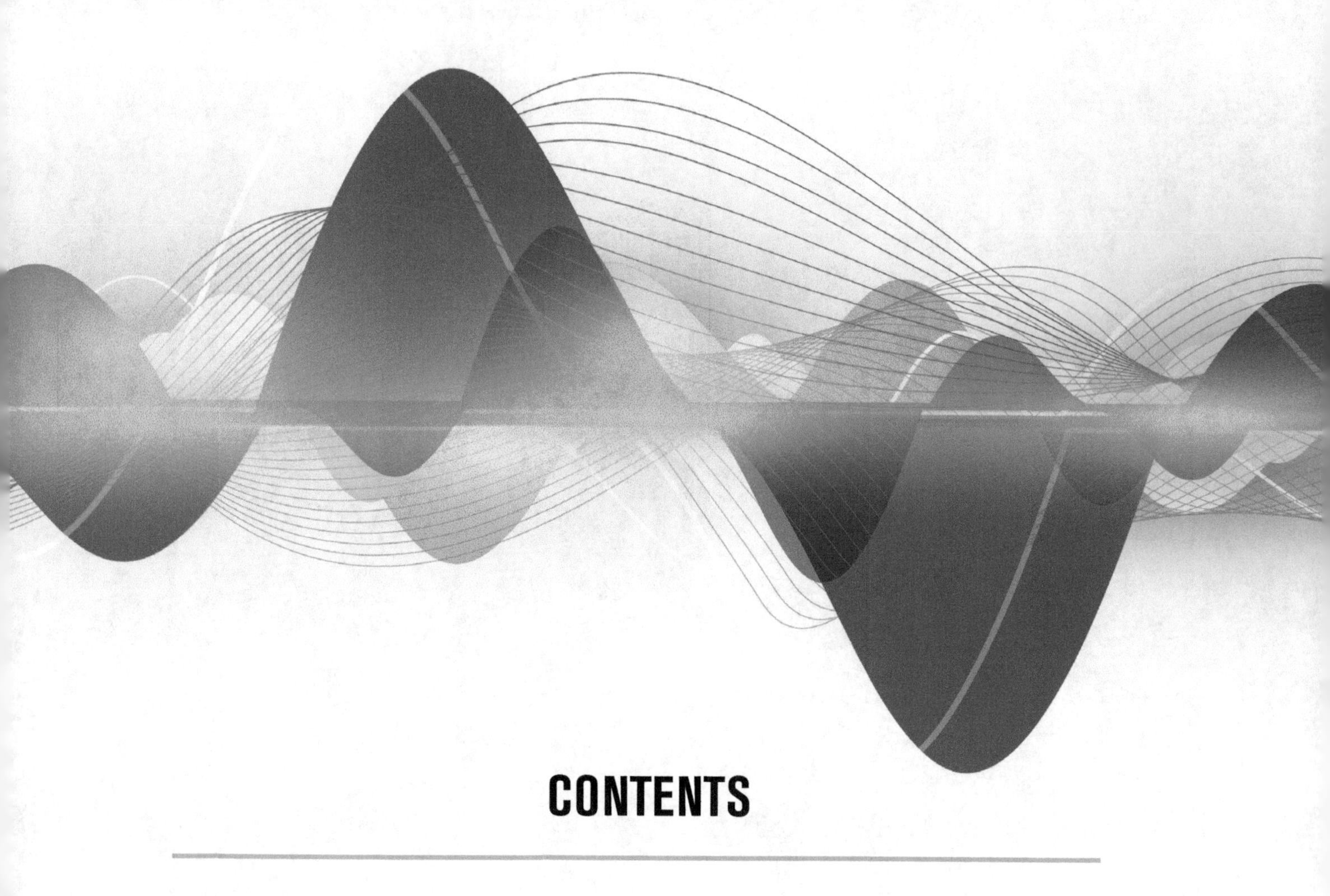

CONTENTS

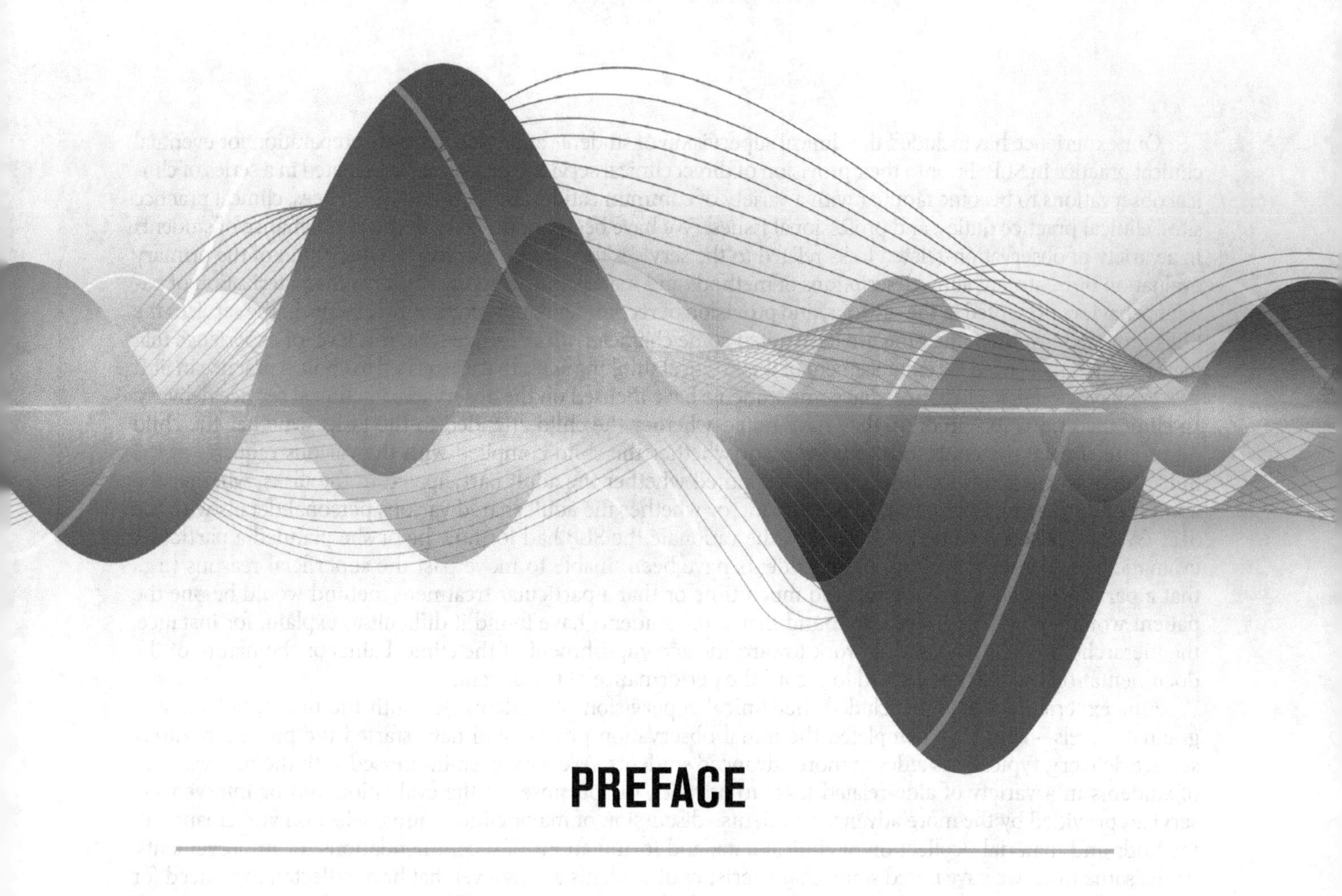

PREFACE

We are speech-language pathologists (SLPs) who have devoted a substantial portion of our professional careers to the provision of services to patients who have presented with a diverse collection of communication disorders and have been in need of our experience and expertise in the course of evaluation, intervention, and consultation services.

What a joy we have experienced when a child with a notable delay in communication development who has never produced a conventional word has at last spoken the name of a favorite individual or a favorite item. What a sense of satisfaction we have experienced when an adult who has lost a substantial amount of expressive communication after a stroke has combined words into a request that family members can understand with ease. What a joy we have experienced when a teen whose physical movements have been compromised by a condition such as cerebral palsy has mastered the intricacies of an alternative communication device that allows the production of functional phrases that convey a variety of content. What a sense of satisfaction we have experienced when an adult with breakdowns in speech fluency has applied such methods as speech rate adjustment in contexts outside a clinic to diminish the impact of stuttered speech on interactions. And, what a pleasure we have found when parents, spouses, and adult children or our patients have found clinical reports and other documentation more palatable because of our explanations of terms and have become less intimated by the clinical process because of our support. These are but a few of the many examples that have exemplified what our opportunities to provide direct services delivery have meant in our lives.

We have treasured these opportunities that we have had to serve our patients and their families. However, over time, we have also come to understand that our contributions to their lives have not been restricted to our direct service delivery to them. That is, we have complemented our clinical endeavors with our clinical education endeavors in that, not only have we provided clinical services, we have also participated extensively in the pre-professional and professional education of the SLPs who may also address their needs in the present or some future point. It is our experiences with these clinical education endeavors that have led us to the point of the preparation of this book.

Our experience has included the clinical supervision of students at the start of their preparation for eventual clinical practice in SLP. Prior to their provision of direct clinical services, they have participated in a series of clinical observations to become familiar with a variety of communication disorders and differences, clinical practice sites, clinical practice duties, and professional issues. We have been impressed with the performance of students in a variety of observation-related tasks related to the services they have observed: identification of the primary evaluation or treatment aims, descriptions of methods and materials used in the sessions, characterization of patient behaviors presented in the sessions, and provision of recommendations for improvements in the services the SLPs provided. At the same time, we have noted some characteristics of students at this level of experience that have reflected their need for enhancement of their critical thinking skills that are related to clinical practice in SLP.

We have noted, for instance, that some students have focused on the observable in clinical service delivery. In clinical sessions for children, they have noted whether the child attended to the tasks, whether the child found the clinical materials to be enjoyable, or whether the child complied with the various requests of the SLP. In clinical sessions for adults, they have noted whether the adult participated in the tasks, whether the adult found the clinical materials to be relevant, or whether the adult shared various personal details with the SLP. We have also noted that, when asked the rationale the SLP had for how he or she planned a particular evaluation or treatment session, some students have been unable to move past the superficial reasons (e.g., that a particular test would not take too much time or that a particular treatment method would be one the patient would enjoy). We have also found that some students have found it difficult to explain, for instance, the hierarchy the SLP has used to work toward the accomplishment of the clinical aims or the nature of the documentation the SLP has created to record the performance of the patient.

Our experience has also included the clinical supervision of students—at both the undergraduate and graduate levels—who have completed the initial observation process and have started the process of direct service delivery, typically as aides to more advanced students. We have been impressed with the performance of students in a variety of aide-related tasks to advance the purposes of the evaluation and/or intervention services provided by the more advanced students: discussion of major clinical aims, selection and creation of methods and materials, collection of clinical data, and formulations of recommendations for improvements. At the same time, we have noted some characteristics of students at this level that have reflected their need for enhancement of their critical thinking skills that will allow them to move effectively into their eventual role as the person primarily responsible for SLP services.

We have observed, in some cases, a rather narrow viewpoint that has influenced the preparations for clinical services. When asked to assist the primary clinician in the preparation of a treatment session, for instance, these students have focused on the amount of time allotted for the session and how much time each of the potential activities would take, with attention to what combination of activities would most closely match the time allotted. When asked to take the lead on one or more activities, these students have used the primary criteria of what is the most familiar, what is the least complicated, and what is the easiest to implement and document to select the activities. After the provision of clinical services, these students, when asked to evaluate the quality of the sessions, have focused as much on their own comfort level and performance as they have on the comfort level and performance of their patients. They have also found it difficult to explain why a patient experienced difficulty with specific activities and how the primary clinician could or should have adjusted the activities to more closely align with the goals of the session. They have, in general, demonstrated inconsistent applications of information to the clinical context and various needs of their patients.

Our experience has included the clinical supervision of students—at both the undergraduate and graduate levels—who have moved past their roles as aides and into those—under close supervision— who are responsible for the preparation, implementation, and documentation of evaluations and intervention sessions. We have been impressed with the performance of students as they have moved from patients with uncomplicated to patients with labyrinthine presentations, from patients with frequently encountered to patients with rarely observed conditions, and from on-campus to off-campus contexts. At the same time, we have noted some characteristics of students at this level that have reflected their need for enhancement of their critical thinking skills that will allow them to more appropriately translate science into practice and judiciously apply their information from the classroom into the clinical sphere.

We have noted a preference on the part of many students to focus on clinical procedures themselves rather than the theoretical foundations for those procedures. A common observation of students has been that academic coursework that includes studies of theories of particular phenomena spend time on theories that could be better spent in instruction on the methods and materials related to clinical service delivery for the population studied in the coursework. The preference for the "how to" over the "why to" approach clinical sessions has been clear. We have also noted that many students are most comfortable with templates that supervisors provide for them. These templates take a variety of forms for such aspects of clinical service delivery as evaluation reports, treatment reports, long-term goals, short-term goals, session plans, session notes, and conferences with patients and their families. A common frustration of students has been that each of their supervisors has a particular way that he or she advises students to prepare such documents and that the students must too frequently adjust to these variations in style. While convenient, templates and "how to" directions are not entirely conducive to enhance critical thinking skills.

Our experience has also included the supervision of clinical fellows, those who have earned their undergraduate and graduate degrees and are immersed in the move toward clinical independence and the acquisition of state and national clinical credentials. We have been impressed with the performance of fellows as they have transformed from neophytes to those capable of more nuanced, proficient clinical performances. At the same time, however, we have noted some characteristics of fellows that we have noted in students that have spoken to their need to realize their entry into professional practice is not a conclusion but rather a commencement of a lifelong need for continued professional development to maintain critical thinking commensurate with their attainment of a graduate degree.

The transition into the clinical fellowship period is, by definition, a multifaceted experience. Those who very recently were students are now practitioners who, while still under supervision, assume over time increased levels of professional leadership for the clinical services they provide, with their supervisors in the role of consultants rather than controllers of the clinical process. Coupled with the need to adapt to a new context and culture, as well as to act in accordance with expectations for clinical service delivery models, clinical documentation, and the many other dimensions of clinical practice, new clinical fellows are understandably overwhelmed. In response to the demands from so many directions, they may rely on the approaches that increase their chances of professional survival and success. The implementation of clinical "recipes" is one such approach that, at least in their view, spares them the need for critical exploration of clinical issues when their time to do such is limited from the start. In fact, their position as fellow and thus as the newest members of the staff of a clinic may have inhibited their desire to introduce critical evaluations of not only the needs of their patients but also the conditions within the clinics where they work.

Our experience has included work in clinical administration, which has allowed us to work collaboratively with experienced clinicians who are sometimes themselves the supervisors of clinical students and clinical fellows. We have been impressed with the dedication of these clinicians to both the art and the science of clinical practice, as well as for their devotion to the thousands of patients with communication disorders whom they have served. At the same time, however, we have noted some characteristics of these talented individuals for whom we have served as administrators that have—in some cases—compromised their continued professional development and service.

At professional conferences, we have been admittedly perplexed by the responses of fellow attendees, some of whom have shown overt disdain for the philosophical over the practical. The thoughts of one attendee whose words we overheard on the plane ride home reflected this view, as she bemoaned the fact that the presenters of one session "wasted so much time on the theory of why we should do this" rather than "tell us what we need to know, which is what to do and how to do it." Such sentiments are unfortunately not isolated but are, at least in our experience, pervasive, as the idea that a master's level education reflects that one can place and interpret experiences within a variety of theoretical contexts is more frequently rejected in favor of the idea that a master's level education reflects simply that one possesses advanced technical clinical skills. The vast number of clinical seminars that focus on practice materials and methods alone, combined with the wealth of clinical materials that sacrifice sound theoretical frameworks for what is colorful, creative, and cost effective, further exacerbates the situation. Even clinicians with a wealth of experience across contexts are sadly not immune to the temptation to embrace what is the easiest to do.

We want to reassure you, our reader, that we ourselves share the need to continue to develop as critical thinkers. In fact, our desire to enhance our own competence in the critical evaluation of professional literature and professional standards and practices has been a primary motivator of our commitment to this topic. Only when we ourselves have the competence to model the attitudes and actions of critical thinkers can we contribute to the development of these attributes in others. Toward this end, we have prepared this book with the hope that those who share our concern for individuals with communication disorders—from the student observer to the seasoned practitioner—will benefit.

In Part 1 of this book, we focus on the mandates for critical thinking from across realms to justify why this practice is so very crucial to successful navigation of the many dimensions of life. In Part 2, we survey the variety of definitions of critical thinking contained in the literature, as well as the various models that scholars have conceived to describe the intricacies of this process. In Part 3, we shift from a philosophical to a practical mode as we describe a system that we have created for the evaluation of critical thinking. We overview the five specific dimensions of critical thinking that we have incorporated into our evaluation: information, innovation, interpretation, integration, and intentionality, as well as the four levels of critical thinking as related to each of these dimensions. We describe how we have applied this framework in the clinical education process, as well as how you, our reader, can incorporate this framework into your clinical practice and administration, as needed. We then provide you with some typical patient referral scenarios for both evaluation and treatment services and explain how you can use these for the evaluation of the level of critical thinking demonstrated by students and practitioners alike. We conclude with some implications of our work for clinical education and some future directions that research in critical thinking in clinical practice in SLP could take. It is our fervent hope that you, our reader, will find this book helpful in your own professional development as you prepare to continue to serve individuals with communication disorders and their families as effectively and compassionately as possible.

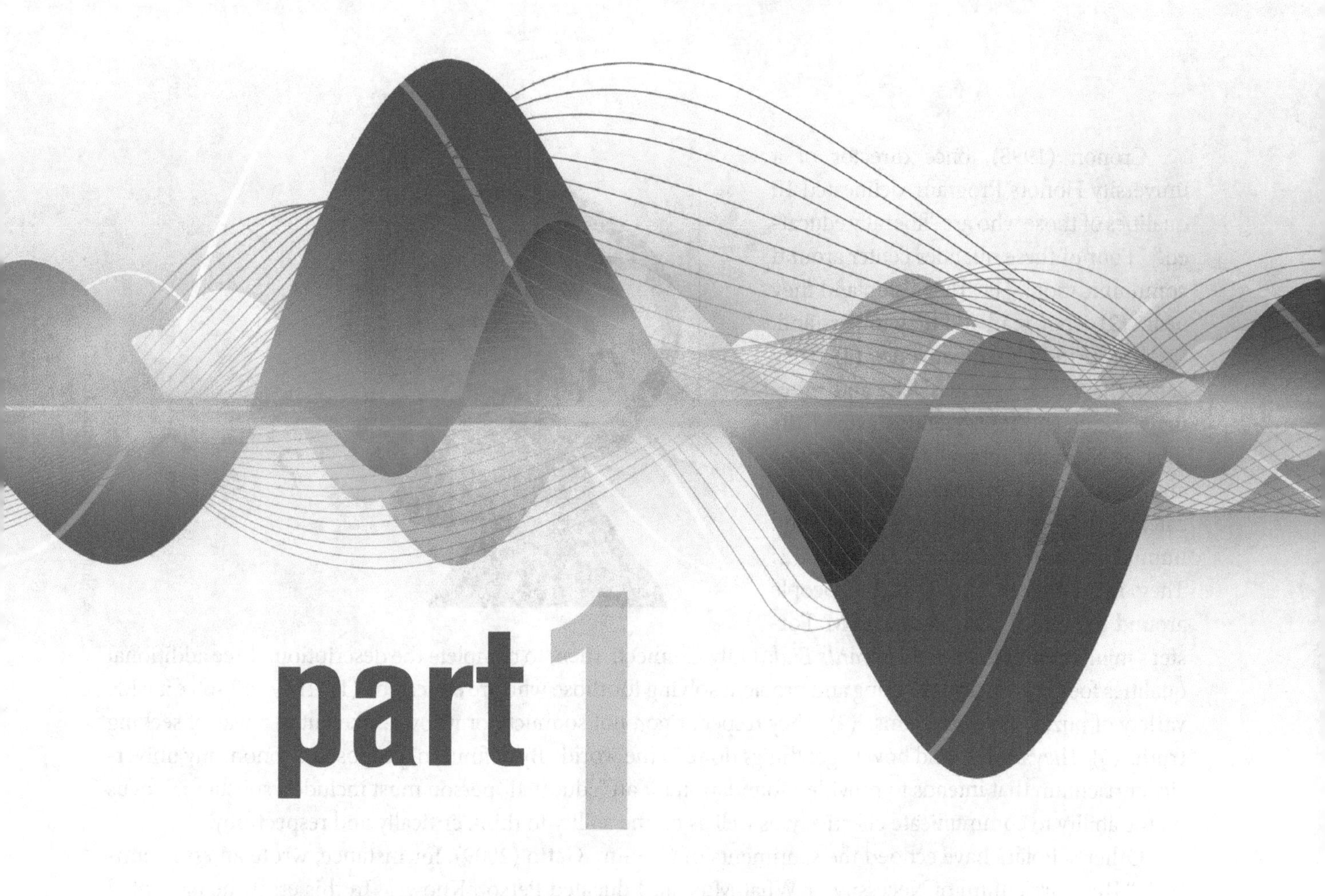

part 1

THE MANDATE FOR CRITICAL THINKING

We live in an era in which the term "critical thinking" confronts us at every turn. From professors to reporters to supervisors to parents, an appeal for improvement in critical thinking rings loudly and clearly. In this section, we explore the nature of this call for institutions and instruction to bring critical thinking into the forefront of our efforts.

In the Educational Realm . . .

A well-known, early 20th-century proponent of continuous improvement in the educational process, Dewey (1910) promoted the classical viewpoint that educators should consider the core of their endeavors to be the nurture of the scientific attitude of the mind. Toward this end, a number of scholars have attempted to delineate what characterizes an "educated" person. We now include a representative sample of these proposed traits of one who is "educated."

Cronon (1998), once director of a university Honors Program, delineated 10 qualities of those who are "liberally educated." Four of these qualities center around communication: (1) They listen and they hear. (2) They read and they understand. (3) They can talk with anyone. (4) They can write clearly, persuasively, and movingly. Three of these qualities extend the idea of communication into connections and relationships for those who are educated: (1) They practice with respect and humility, tolerance and self-criticism. (2) They nurture and empower the people around them. (3) They follow E. M. Forster's injunction in the novel *Howard's End*: Only Connect. Then, to complete the description, three additional qualities focus on critical thinking and problem solving for those who are educated: (1) They can solve a wide variety of puzzles and problems. (2) They respect rigor, not so much for its own sake but as a way of seeking truth. (3) They understand how to get things done in the world. By definition, proposed Cronon, any university curriculum that intends to provide a foundation for an "educated" person must include a substantial focus on the ability to communicate effectively, as well as on the ability to think critically and respectfully.

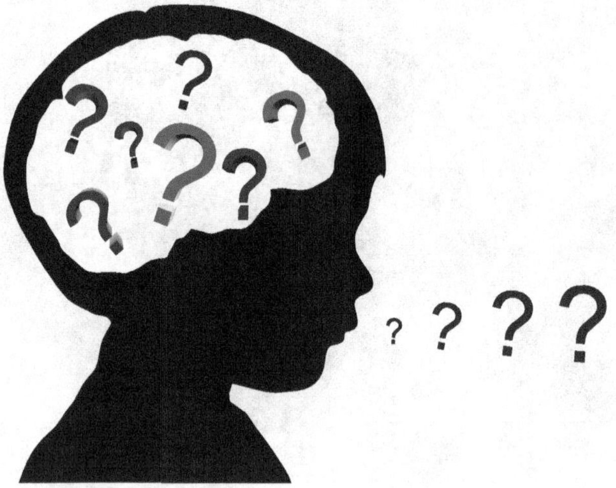

Other scholars have echoed the sentiments of Cronin. Gatto (2009), for instance, wrote an essay entitled, "The Curriculum of Necessity or What Must an Educated Person Know?" In this essay, he presented a list of qualities for successful transition from academic into a career that a division within Harvard University purportedly distributed to its students. Each of these qualities, in some way, reflects a dimension of critical thinking: the ability to (a) define problems without a guide, (b) attack problems heuristically, (c) ask hard questions which challenge prevailing assumptions, (d) quickly assimilate needed data from masses of irrelevant information, (e) conceptualize and reorganize information into new patterns, (f) discuss ideas with an eye toward application, (g) think inductively, deductively, and dialectically, (h) work in teams without guidance, (i) work absolutely alone, and (j) persuade others that your course is the right one. Some of these qualities also tapped into the aforementioned need for effective communication and respectful interaction simultaneously with the search for the best possible solutions. Gatto, after he listed these qualities, noted that he did not believe that schools, as a matter of policy, teach these traits but rather promoted ways to teach people how to be dependent. He called for this situation to be soon corrected.

In his essay, Kaufman (2011), in response to the list provided by Gatto, created a list of what he called "Core Human Skills." This list reflected the lists of Cronon and Gatto in some respects. With respect to communication, Kaufman noted the value of "rapport," or interaction with others, and the value of "conflict resolution," or anticipation of and resolutions for disagreements. He also listed both "writing" and "speaking" clearly and concisely as essential. With respect to relationships, he focused upon informational relationships rather than personal relationships with his focus on "information assimilation" (the consumption and comprehension of information most relevant to a problem), "scenario generation" (the creation and evaluation of potential future scenarios), "planning" (the identification of the next steps to achieve an aim), "decision-making" (the identification and establishment of priorities for information and the avoidance of common informational errors), and "interrelation" (the comprehension of key features of systems and relationships, such as cause and effect). He also noted the specific discipline of mathematics as quite useful in the process of interpretation of information. To enhance his list, Kaufman also noted aspects of self, such as "self-awareness" (the perception of and influence over one's own internal state) and "skill acquisition" (how one acquires competence via access of resources, deconstruction of complex processes, and active experimentation).

In addition to these "core values," Kaufman provided a list of core skills of an educated person that a division within Princeton University purportedly distributed to its students. This list was similar to the previous lists. The idea of "communication" appeared in the ability to "think, speak, and write clearly." The idea of "critical thinking" appeared in the ability to "reason critically and systematically," "conceptualize and solve problems," "think independently," and see "different modes of thought (including quantitative, historical, scientific, and aesthetic)." The idea of relationships appeared in the ability to "take initiative and work independently," and "work in cooperation with others and learn collaboratively." This list also spoke of how an individual interacts with information, as in the ability to "judge what it means to understand something thoroughly," "distinguish the important from the trivial, the enduring from the ephemeral," and "see connections among disciplines, ideas, and cultures." The list also noted the need for a "depth of knowledge in a particular field" and a "commitment to lifelong learning." Kaufman further posited that a consensus exists about what it means to be an "educated" person, or one who is equipped to deal with common life situations. He also noted that "education" is a continuous process not synonymous with the process of qualification for academic and professional credentials. In short, education does not end when school ends.

McGregor (2010), in his treatise on the characteristics of an educated person, echoed this theme when he noted, "Education is not about certificates and degrees; education is about how a person relates to life (n.p.)." He further noted, "Education is the opposite of indoctrination. Indoctrination tells people what to think, tells people what the 'truth' is, closes minds to critical thought (n.p.)." He characterized education as about learning, not teaching, and noted that education "opens the mind, encourages a search for truth, and develops a mind that can engage critically with many different ideas." He characterized educated persons as those who (a) have empathy and strive to understand others as they withhold their own judgment until they are sure that they understand, (b) are sensitive to the psychological, physical, moral, and cultural milieu in which they find themselves and remain respectful, (c) understand clearly their own values, wants, and preferences without the desire to impose these on others, (d) are independent within the constraints of collaborative life and take responsibility for themselves, (e) understand the connectedness of all that is in the world and act responsibly, and (f) are congruent and comfortable with themselves.

In a different approach, Mohanan (2005) described what he called the "ingredients of educatedness." He started with the idea of the knowledge that a person possesses, which he further divided into "general" versus "specialized" knowledge, "universal" versus "culture specific" knowledge, and "foundational" and "non-foundational" knowledge. He also stressed the difference between "declarative memory" (i.e., to know <u>that</u>) and "procedural memory" (i.e., to know <u>how</u>). To attain this level of competence with information, Mohanan noted the need for various skills. He described "thinking abilities" as both generalized and specialized in nature and required for making "informed intelligent decisions, estimates, assessments, and inferences." He described "learning abilities" as independent learning that "facilitates coping with and adapting to the changing environment." He then described "language abilities" as those skills that enable one to use language "clearly, precisely, and effectively for epistemic purposes." He then delineated various "mind set qualities" as an awareness of the uncertainty of knowledge, the willingness to deal with degrees of uncertainty and to doubt and question propositions that are claimed as knowledge, as well as an openness of mind for that allows modification of knowledge based on new or revised evidence, a personal involvement in knowledge as a set of beliefs, and an intellectual curiosity that leads to enjoyment of knowledge, thinking, and learning in themselves.

Mohanan noted that these properties of the mind cannot be brought about by explicit instruction, but instead with the proper educational environment and educational role models. He further noted, "Among the qualities mentioned above, the ability to subject one's own beliefs to the process of critical thinking requires special emphasis. Critical thinking requires the capacity and predilection to seek rational grounds for accepting or rejecting beliefs (n.p.)." He then proceeded to specify three successively difficult levels in critical scrutiny of beliefs: (1) What kind of rational grounds would support my beliefs and refute my opponent's beliefs? (2) What kinds of rational grounds would justify my acceptance or rejection of the beliefs that I am exposed to? (3) What kind of rational grounds would refute my beliefs and support my opponent's beliefs? Each reflects increasingly more sophisticated critical thinking.

In additional reflections on the topic, Sparks (2010), in his essay, "What It Means to Be an Educated Person," presented his qualities of an educated person as these relate to future education and/or employment. These included the fact that education enables students to discover their talents and passions and link those to ways that enrich their own lives and the lives of others. These also included the fact that education helps students understand how they learn best so that they can remain employable across their life spans. These points are complemented by the idea that education stimulates lifelong curiosity and creativity and provides the civic skills and attitudes required to sustain a vibrant democracy. An ultimate aim of education is that a student has the skills and the disposition to be successful at whatever comes next in life, as well as the attitudes and the resourcefulness that promote hope rather than despair. Toward this end, students must appreciate diversity and acquire the interpersonal skills that enable productivity.

In his book *Assessment for Excellence*, Astin (1991) asserted, "of all the skills that are considered basic to the purposes of a liberal education, critical thinking is probably at the top of the list" (p. 47). Lampert (2007) noted that "critical thinking is generally considered to be a desirable outcome of an undergraduate liberal arts education" (p. 17). Mead (2010), in her essay "Learning by Degrees," in *The New Yorker*, noted an education is "to nurture critical thought; to expose individuals to the signal accomplishments of humankind; to develop in them an ability not just to listen actively but to respond intelligently." Giancarlo and Facione (2001) reflected that, "teaching for thinking has always been central to the very concept of a liberal education" (p. 17) and that "educators must commit to sharpening students' cognitive skills and strengthening their disposition toward critical thinking" (p. 18). Taken as a whole, these views promote the development of critical thinking as a central motivation for and outcome of study.

The mission statements adopted by academic institutions across the nation have incorporated the centrality of the development of critical thinking into these inspirational and aspirational proclamations of their aims. While many of these statements do not specifically use the term "critical thinking," the spirit of these statements frequently alludes to this concept. Here are selected examples of mission statements from the vast number of such statements available.

Statements from pre-college and university schools (elementary and secondary) have noted the value of critical thinking, as well as the importance of the earliest possible introduction to experiences that promote this concept. We have selected but a sample of these mission statements from across the nation to demonstrate the widespread embrace of critical thinking as central to the institutional purposes and the educational curricula that these inspire.

© Shutterstock/JavanovicDejan

From private institutions . . .

From the Mountain and Plains States . . .

The Colorado Academy, Colorado (n.d.): ". . . Here, we turn ideals into action – challenging our students to become lifelong learners, thinkers, inquisitors, and contributors . . . We emphasize our Six Cs of 21st Century skills: Critical Thinking and Problem Solving, Communication, Collaboration, Creativity, Cultural Competence, and Character Development."

From the East Coast . . .

The William Penn Charter School, Pennsylvania (n.d.): ". . . We value scholarship and inquiry. With excellence as our standard, we challenge students in a vigorous program of academics, arts, and athletics. Through global connections, civic engagement and a focus on environmental sustainability, we inspire students to be thinkers, collaborators, innovators, and leaders. We educate students to live lives that make a difference."

From the West Coast . . .

Within the second area, students will "make connections in content and integrate knowledge; consider multiple points of view and generate alternate solutions; evaluate information and predict consequences; acquire, assess, and organize information from a variety of sources; read, write, listen, and speak with comprehension and clarity; (and) incorporate the visual and performing arts as expressive communication strategies."

Van Nuys High School, California (n.d.): "Van Nuys High School is committed to creating a secure and safe environment where students will become academically capable and self-sufficient individuals, effective communicators, critical and analytical thinkers, self-directed lifelong learners, and responsible and ethical citizens."

From the Southeast . . .

Hume-Fogg Magnet High School, Tennessee (n.d.): "Our mission is to ENGAGE, EQUIP, and EMPOWER the academically talented and culturally diverse students we serve (and to) engage them in a challenging college preparatory program of study, equip them with the knowledge and skills necessary for success, (and) empower them to be people of courage, compassion, and character . . . Our program promotes high academic standards through both independent and cooperative learning formats. We encourage creative thinking, abstract reasoning, self-discipline, integrity, public service, and pursuit of individual interests."

These statements, taken as a whole and as representative of academic institutions across the nation, underscore the value placed upon critical thinking as a cornerstone for the missions of institutions and as the inspiration for the curricula promoted by these institutions. Statements from universities and colleges further affirm the mission of educational institutions to continue to promote critical thinking across both curricular and co-curricular endeavors.

From private institutions . . .

From the Mountain and Plains States . . .

The University of Denver, Colorado (n.d.): ". . . We strive to empower greatness in our students . . . Every student benefits from an innovative curriculum that emphasizes writing, quantitative reasoning, experiential learning, and cross-disciplinary inquiry."

From the Southeast . . .

Wake Forest University, North Carolina (n.d.): "Wake Forest University aspires to . . . link intellectual curiosity, moral reflection, and a commitment to service, shaping ethically informed leaders to serve humanity."

From public institutions . . .

From the West Coast . . .

The University of California System (n.d.): "The distinctive mission of the University is to serve society as a center of higher learning, providing long-term societal benefits through transmitting advanced knowledge, discovering new knowledge, and functioning as an active working repository of organized knowledge. That obligation, more specifically, includes undergraduate education, graduate and professional education, research, and other kinds of public service, which are shaped and bounded by the central pervasive mission of discovering and advancing knowledge."

From the Midwest . . .

Iowa State University (2014): ". . . We must prepare the leaders of our nation and the world . . . To create knowledge, Iowa State must be a magnet for attracting outstanding students, faculty, and staff who will learn, work, and conduct world-class research and scholarship that address the challenges of the 21st century. To share knowledge, Iowa State's faculty, staff, and students must be able to communicate with and learn from diverse populations. The University must maintain a strong focus on student success and provide exceptional undergraduate, graduate, professional, and outreach programs that prepare students and citizens for leadership and success. To apply knowledge, Iowa State's faculty, staff, and students must be able to develop global partnerships to convert what they know into products, services, and information that will improve the quality of life for the citizens of Iowa, the nation, and the world."

These statements, once more taken as a whole and as representative of academic institutions across the nation, underscore the value placed upon critical thinking as a cornerstone for the missions of institutions and as the inspiration for the curricula promoted by these institutions. However, while enrichment of critical thinking has been the ideal, evidence exists to document that academic institutions have collectively fallen woefully short of the attainment of this ideal.

Kurfiss (1988) conceptualized critical thinking as a variation of "higher-order cognition that society requires and faculty esteem" (p. 1). To complement this sentiment, Gardiner (2013) noted, "Many of us believe our society would function far more wisely, harmoniously, and safely in a complex, ever more rapidly changing, and dangerous world if leaders and citizens used critical thinking more consistently than they now do" (p. 123). In a contradiction of this sentiment, however, Gardiner noted, in reality, many students have not attained the ideal of consistent critical thinking. In fact, he conceptualized students as "dualists" who have seen the world in fixed dichotomies and "multiplists" who have not appreciated the construction of meaning that is realized by the process of critical thinking.

Yanklowitz (2013) lamented that most entry-level students at universities today are weak in critical thinking skills. Research has documented this pattern, as when Perie, Grigg, and Donahue (2005) reported that fewer than 10% of Grade 12 students could make informed, critical judgments about written text and that only 15% of these students could write well-structured argumentative essays. Cuban (2010), well known for his critique of the educational process, noted that the current view of education is a narrow one: "That . . . says a good education is one where a school (note that schooling and education become one) . . . meets state curriculum standards, has satisfactory test scores, and moves all students successfully to the next level of schooling" (n.p.). The attainment of narrow standards, coupled with the attainment of scores above a specified criterion, need not be equated (and, in fact, probably should not be equated) with the acquisition of skills for success, central to which is critical thinking. Barr and Tagg (1995) reflected the continuation of this perspective—that "schooling" and "being educated" are one—into university-level education as they described a philosophical shift in university-level instruction from successful "teaching" to successful "learning." The current measurements of educational outcomes have not necessarily tapped into the skills that are indicative of a critical and/or creative thinker who is successful as a problem solver.

In their book *Academically Adrift: Limited Learning on College Campuses*, Arum and Roksa (2011) asserted that students at universities show no substantial improvements in their critical thinking skills over time. They measured the critical thinking skills of over 2,300 students across 24 academic institutions with the "Performance Task" section of the Collegiate Learning Assessment (CLA) tool (2006), which required that students provide written responses to a prompt inspired by a realistic situation. They obtained data at the commencement of Year 1 and Year 2 in which these students were enrolled and reported that these data indicated no substantial improvements in critical thinking of 45% of the students whom they reviewed. They also obtained data at the conclusion of Year 2 (Arum, Roksa, & Cho, 2010) and reported that these additional data indicated no substantial improvements in critical thinking in 36% of students whom they reviewed. These scholars implicated both individuals—students and faculty—and institutional cultures as culprits in the fact that university-level studies have not been conducive to the development in critical thinking for a notable proportion of students. Paul, Elder, and Bartell (1997) studied 38 public and 28 private institutions in California to address the question of whether future teachers were prepared to teach critical thinking. The faculty of these institutions asserted that their instruction was permeated with critical thinking opportunities, which led to successful instruction of their students. In contrast, however, the majority of these faculty could not clearly explain the concept of critical thinking, misconstrued their teaching methods as enhancing critical thinking, failed to delineate critical thinking standards they established for students, and failed to list specific critical thinking tasks and traits. In his subsequent reflections of critical thinking in university-level studies, Paul (2004) also implicated faculty members in the decline of this skill in students. In fact, he concluded that research supported the ideas that faculty members themselves have not framed their instruction within the concept of critical thinking, have not realized that they themselves do not understand the depth and breadth of this topic, and have believed, in fact, that their instruction has contributed to the development of critical thinking in students.

Given that the results of this seminal research describe the present status of critical thinking in university-level students and portray the need for continued emphasis upon the development of students as thinkers in university-level studies, we assert that the creation and implementation of tools to facilitate this development is crucial.

In the professional realm . . .

Within professional disciplines exists a variety of documents that codify the ethical standards that underscore practice in those disciplines. SLP is not alone in our embrace of a "Code of Ethics." While such codes are not identical across disciplines, they share core themes that capture the values that practitioners hold dear. Within the SLP Code of Ethics (2010r) are themes that are reflected in codes of our sister disciplines: (a) paramount concern for the welfare of those whom we serve professionally, (b) commitment to the maintenance and enhancement of professional competence, (c) accurate representation of information about the profession and clinical service delivery to those influenced by the discipline, (d) development and maintenance of harmonious, respectful professional relationships, and (e) promotion of the mission and maintenance of accountability for the professional standards of the discipline. Opportunities for application of critical thinking skills are inherent and mandated in each of these ethical precepts.

Theme (a): Paramount Concern for the Welfare of Those Whom We Serve Professionally.

In 2002, three associations—the American Board of Internal Medicine (ABIM) Foundation, the American College of Physicians Foundation, and the European Federation of Internal Medicine—created and published a "physician charter." This three-pronged charter, endorsed by over 100 medical and dental associations around the world, captured the fundamental ideas of concern for individuals in need of medical services. The principle of "primacy of patient welfare" reflects a dedication of the professional to serve the interest of the patient, with altruism central to the trust that forms the provider–patient relationship. Further, the principle of "patient autonomy" demands honesty from provider to patient that leads to patient empowerment to enact informed decisions about ethical, appropriate care. Finally, the principle of "social justice" reflects the promotion of fair and equitable distribution of health care to individuals regardless of their personal characteristics. While created by medical professionals, this "charter" is equally applicable to practitioners across complementary health care disciplines and reflects core ideas that these disciplines promote. While each of these "prongs" demands application of critical thinking skills, the second principle—that of patient autonomy—provides even more stringent demands, as providers work with their patients to determine whether, based on available evidence, proposed services meet the criteria for "ethical" and "appropriate." Certainly, as SLPs, we have promoted the welfare of those whom we have served professionally as an extension of the care for individuals with communication disorders (and their families) that led to our pursuit of SLP for our vocation.

Theme (b): Commitment to the Maintenance and Enhancement of Professional Competence.

Epstein and Hundert (2002) noted that, for medical practitioners, evaluation of professional competence focused upon two dimensions, core scientific information and basic practice skills. In response to this tradition, they proposed a more inclusive definition of competence, "the habitual and judicious use of communication, knowledge, technical skills, clinical reasoning, emotions, values, and reflection in daily practice for the benefit of the individual and the community being served" (p. 226). They posited that "competence builds on a foundation of basic clinical skills, scientific knowledge, and moral development" (p. 226). Competence, according to Epstein and Hundert, involves a cognitive function—acquiring and using knowledge to solve real-life problems —as well as an integrative function (using data in clinical reasoning), a relational function (communicating effectively with patients and colleagues), and an affective/moral function (the willingness, patience, and emotional awareness to use skills judiciously and humanely) (p. 227). Competence, according to Epstein and Hundert, further depends on habits of mind, including attentiveness, critical curiosity, self-awareness, and presence (p. 228). And, to advance professional development in these areas, they proposed new approaches to evaluation of professional competence: clinical reasoning, expert judgment, management of ambiguity, professionalism, time management, learning strategies, and teamwork (p. 229) that are facilitated by institutional support, reflection, and mentoring. Certainly, as SLPs, we have shared the commitment to advance our professional competence for both philosophical and practical reasons.

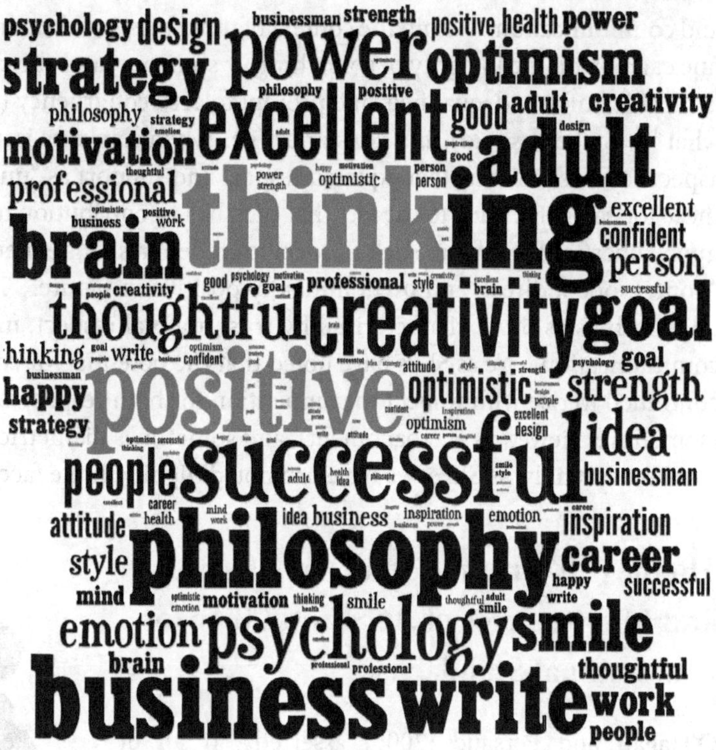

© Shutterstock/meanep

Theme (c): Accurate Representation of Information about the Profession and Clinical Service Delivery.

By definition, the presentation of information from providers and patients to each other is a mutual process influenced by various factors: those related to the provider, those related to the mode of communication, and those related to the patient (Ley, 1988). Because of this, multiple sources of potential miscommunication exist that can influence the perceptions of providers and patients of each other, as well as the effectiveness of the evaluation and treatment processes. Tang and Newcomb (1998) developed a set of guidelines, the P.A.T.I.E.N.T. Guide, which reflects the concern of practitioners that the information that they distribute complement rather than confuse patient care. The P.A.T.I.E.N.T. acronym reflects Personal, Articulate, Timely, Informative, Endorsed, Next-Step, and Therapeutic information dissemination guidelines. "Personal" reflects the need for patients to have access to specific information about their health, while "Articulate" references the relationship between clarity of information and its believability and applicability. "Timely" reflects the need for permanent information provided in an efficient fashion whenever questions arise, while "Informative" references the relationship between individuality of information and sensitivity to literacy and other potential communication barriers that exist. "Endorsed" reflects the need for information that is accepted by authoritative sources, while "Next-Step" references the need for concise and explicit care-related instructions. Finally, "Therapeutic" notes the value of mechanisms to improve comprehension and retention of information and instructions to enhance compliance with the service delivery process. Robinson (2002) delineated the principles of acceptance, validation, empathy, respect, and advocacy as crucial in effective provider–patient communication. Certainly, as SLPs, we have strived to promote the professional nature of our discipline with accurate information that we have explained as clearly as possible based upon the needs of our various audiences.

Theme (d): Development and Maintenance of Respectful, Harmonious Professional Relationships.

Manion (2011) described four elements of the "healthy work relationship." These are trust, respect, support, and communication. Within the context of the professional environment, she equated trust with the fact that one can rely on the integrity of something or someone, and she considered competence (i.e., when someone is capable, informed, qualified, and prompt to act), congruency (i.e., when someone acts in accordance with what he or she has said), and constancy (i.e., when someone is available and accessible) as three important aspects of trust. She further equated respect and support as "unconditional" and noted that others provide these for each other due to the fact that each has a contribution to offer the world (and not necessarily based upon superficial attributes such as specific credentials). She then characterized effective communication as "honest, open, direct, and predominantly positive in nature." Mind Tools (n.d.) defined healthy working relationships as those characterized by trust, mutual respect, mindfulness, welcoming diversity, and open communication. We as SLPs have noted that the potential for conflicts across health-related disciplines has continued to rise with respect to competition for both respect and resources, shared clinical practice issues (sometimes viewed as encroachment), and sometimes diametrically opposed clinical practice philosophies. Even so, certainly, as SLPs, we have promoted dignity in the face of diversity of opinions.

Theme (e): Promotion of the Mission and Maintenance of Accountability for Professional Standards.

O'Hagan and Persaud (2009) asserted, "If an organization wishes to continuously learn and use evidence-based practices, it must create a sense of accountability . . . Instead of shifting from one flavor of the month to the next, accountability ensures the permanence of performance management and continuous improvement by holding people accountable on a daily basis. The totality of all persons being accountable for their actions serves to create accountability at the unit, department, organizational, and industry level" (p. 124). Emmanuel and Emmanuel (1996) defined accountability as "the procedures and processes by which one party justifies and takes responsibility for its activities such as for achieving various organizational

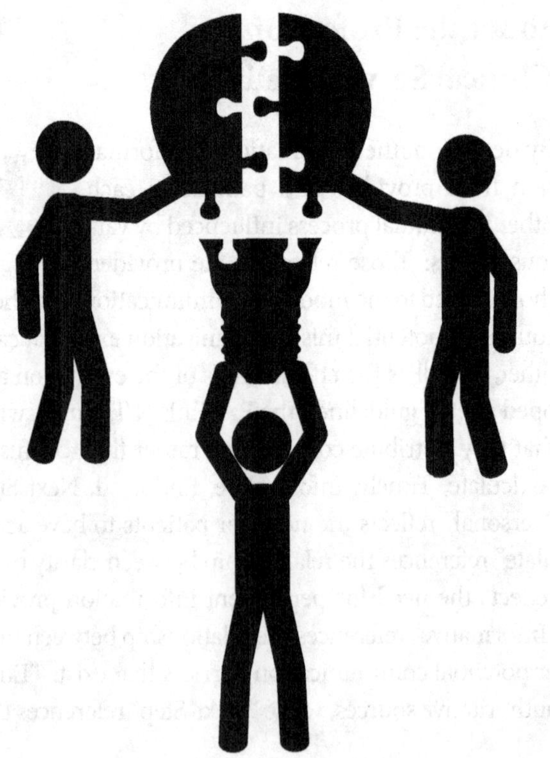

goals" (p. 229). Brinkerhoff (2003) stressed that any definition of accountability should address "accountability for what?" at its core. He noted three general categories of accountability: financial (as in allocation, disbursement, utilization, and documentation of resources), performance (as in quantity and quality of services, outputs, and results), and political/democratic (as in institutions, procedures, and mechanisms that respond to societal needs and concerns). O'Hagan and Persaud (2009) noted several reasons that a "culture of accountability" is vital: improved quality of care; value for funds spent for services; reduction of overuse, misuse, and underuse of resources; increased use of evidence-based practice; reduction of inappropriate care; and continued assessment of evidence from process and outcome measures. Wachter (2012) expanded on this idea with the "Just Culture" model of accountability, which differentiates between the "expected flaws of mortals" and "those transgressions that merit an accountability approach." And, with respect to those "transgressions," Leonard and Frankel (2010) noted several reflection questions to ponder before the imposition of professional sanctions: Was an individual knowingly impaired? Did the individual consciously decide to engage in an unsafe act? Did the individual make a mistake that individuals of similar experience and training would be likely to make under the same circumstances? Does the individual have a history of unsafe acts? Finally, Bell, Delbanco, Anderson-Shaw, McDonald, and Gallagher (2011) noted the tension between "no blame" and "accountability," as well as the tension between "individual" and "collective" accountability at the levels of the individual practitioner, the health care team, and the institution. Donaldson (2001) captured both the letter and the spirit of accountability in his three-component model of this concept: the individual's professional accountability for the quality of his or her own work, the accountability of health professionals within the organizations in which they work, and the accountability (with others) for the organization's performance and its provision of services. Certainly, as has been the case for each principle, we, as SLPs, have aimed to be both individually and collectively accountable for our professional conduct.

The ethical statements from a variety of professional associations with whom SLPs collaboratively provide clinical services reflect these themes, which in turn reflect the necessity for critical thinking. Excerpts from these ethical statements follow to demonstrate the depth and the breadth of the commitment to critical thinking. While certainly not comprehensive, the representative ethical statements that follow implicitly or explicitly support critical thinking.

The American Medical Association (2001): "A physician shall continue to study, apply, and advance scientific knowledge, maintain a commitment to medical education, make relevant information available to patients, colleagues, and the public, obtain consultation, and use the talents of other health professionals when indicated."

The American Nursing Association (2001): "The nurse is responsible and accountable for individual nursing practice and determines the appropriate delegation of tasks consistent with the nurse's obligation to provide optimum patient care . . . The nurse owes the same duties to self as to others, including the responsibility to preserve integrity and safety, to maintain competence, and to continue personal and professional growth."

The American Dental Association (n.d.): "The dentist has a duty to refrain from harming the patient. Interpretation: This principle expresses the concept that professionals have a duty to protect the patient from harm. Under this principle, the dentist's primary obligations include keeping knowledge and skills current, knowing one's own limitations and when to refer to a specialist or other professional, and knowing when and under what circumstances delegation of patient care to auxiliaries is appropriate."

The American Psychological Association (2002): "Psychologists recognize that fairness and justice entitle all persons to access to and benefit from the contributions of psychology and to equal quality in the processes, procedures, and services being conducted by psychologists. Psychologists exercise reasonable judgment and take precautions to ensure that their potential biases, the boundaries of their competence, and the limitations of their expertise do not lead to or condone unjust practices . . . Psychologists' work is based upon established scientific and professional knowledge of the discipline."

The National Association of Social Workers (2008): "Social workers should strive to become and remain proficient in professional practice and the performance of professional functions. Social workers should critically examine and keep current with emerging knowledge relevant to social work. Social workers should routinely review the professional literature and participate in continuing education relevant to social work practice and social work ethics. Social workers should base practice on recognized knowledge, including empirically based knowledge, relevant to social work and social work ethics . . . Social workers should monitor and evaluate policies, the implementation of programs, and practice interventions. Social workers should promote and facilitate evaluation and research to contribute to the development of knowledge. Social workers should critically examine and keep current with emerging knowledge relevant to social work and fully use evaluation and research evidence in their professional practice."

The American Occupational Therapy Association (2010): "Reevaluate and reassess recipients of service in a timely manner to determine if goals are being achieved and whether intervention plans should be revised . . . Use, to the extent possible, evaluation, planning, intervention techniques, and therapeutic equipment that are evidence-based and within the recognized scope of occupational therapy practice . . . Take responsibility for promoting and practicing occupational therapy on the basis of current knowledge and research and for further developing the profession's body of knowledge . . . Avoid compromising client rights or well-being based on arbitrary administrative directives by exercising professional judgment and critical analysis."

The American Physical Therapy Association (n.d.): "Physical therapists shall be accountable for making sound professional judgments . . . Physical therapists shall demonstrate independent and objective professional judgment in the patient's/client's best interest in all practice settings. Physical therapists shall demonstrate professional judgment informed by professional standards, evidence (including current literature and established best practice), practitioner experience, and patient/client values. Physical therapists shall make judgments within their scope of practice and level of expertise and shall communicate with, collaborate with, or refer to peers or other health care professionals when necessary."

The National Education Association (1975): "The educator strives to help each student realize his or her potential as a worthy and effective member of society. The educator therefore works to stimulate the spirit of inquiry, the acquisition of knowledge and understanding, and the thoughtful formulation of worthy goals."

Taken as a whole, these statements of the expected ethical standards of professionals weave the value of critical thinking into every dimension of practice. At the same time, observations from scholars across disciplines remind us of the gap between the aim and the actual. Gambrill (1999), as an example, noted a difference between what is claimed and what is accomplished. What is claimed is that credentials —such as diplomas and licenses—ensure professional competence. What is accomplished, however, may not reflect this claim. To ensure consistency between claim and accomplishment, Gambrill contrasted two approaches to the relationship between content and practice, (a) evidence based and (b) authority based, with a preference for the application of the actual competence that is expected from one who has earned credentials.

In a complementary view, Seymour, Kinn, and Sutherland (2003) noted the presumption that critical thinking skills demonstrated in the classroom transfer into the appraisal and the application of research in clinical practice. They further noted, however, that this transfer does not automatically occur, which results in a disjuncture between research and practice. They recommended that critical and creative thinking are prerequisites to narrow the distance between research and practice and to foster appreciation for both the art and the science of clinical practice.

In another complementary view, Gambrill (2004) discussed the mandate that professionals honor the code of ethics in a profession. She noted that, unfortunately, professionals do not honor these standards in a consistent fashion. She promotes the role of critical thinking in honoring ethical mandates and their relationship to evidence-based practice. In an example of how the aspirations of a discipline translate into educational practices, Maudsley and Strivens (2000) discussed the recommendations of the General Medical Council to define core knowledge in undergraduate medical education, as well as to encourage better application of this knowledge base in clinical judgment, critical thinking, and reflective practice. Core concepts related to preparation of undergraduate medical students for professional practice are comprehension of the scientific foundations of medical practice, the role of understanding and thinking in undergraduate medical education, the transferability of skills to promote competence, and the nature of clinical judgment.

Then, in a further attempt to stress the need for practitioners as thinkers, Vratny and Shriver (2007) described a conceptual model of evidence-based practice (EBF) that supported a culture of quality care, clinical excellence, critical thinking, and professional growth. The model addressed clinician expertise and values, experience, patient preference and expectation, and caring in the establishment of an environment that aimed to become rooted in clinical research and evidence-based practice. The authors asserted that, while education nourished EBP, the qualities of leadership, enthusiasm, mentorship, clinical inquiry, and reflective practice made EBP thrive. Given these and other mandates to close the gap between what is aspirational and what is actual (in terms of accomplishment), critical thinking continues to be a mandatory practice.

In the institutional realm . . .

Pre-professional and professional preparation lead to, for most individuals, positions as clinical practitioners across a variety of medical, rehabilitation, and educational sites. Professional employment is characterized not only by discipline-specific practices but also by the traits that differentiate successful from unsuccessful employees. The literature from the human resources field substantiates the value of critical thinking in workplace success.

© Shutterstock/Login

Mayhew (n.d.) discussed examples of critical thinking in the process of decision making in the workplace. He noted, "Fair-mindedness, complemented by rational decision-making in a reasonable manner that emulates empathy, is a characteristic any employer would be lucky to have in all of its employees" (n.p.). Mayhew presented examples of human resources (e.g., employee decisions), marketing (e.g., decisions regarding public perception of products and services), and customer service (e.g., conflict resolution, satisfactory service) as areas in which application of critical thinking skills can increase the likelihood of rational decision making.

The Society of Human Resources Management (SHRM) and Kaplan University survey findings (2014) indicated that, other than education completed, the skills related to "communication" and "critical thinking" were two of the top three most valuable skill sets for employment applicants. For applicants across disciplines, 94% of employers rated "communication skills" as vital, and 73% of employers rated "critical thinking skills" as vital. An earlier survey (2008) by the SHRM addressed the issues of shortages of skills in the available labor pool. Of human resources professionals who responded to the survey, 58% reported that some workers lack competencies needed to perform their jobs (up from 54% in 2005). Additionally, 55% of the respondents noted that workers who enter the job market in the next decade will lack the competencies for success in the workplace. When asked about the most valuable skills, they cited "employee adaptability" and "critical thinking skills" as the most vital. For experienced workers, 47% of respondents cited adaptability/flexibility, while 41% of respondents cited critical thinking/problem solving as vital. The value of these skills was comparable to their value for novice workers, with 46% of respondents in favor of adaptability/flexibility and 35% of respondents in favor of critical thinking/problem solving as the number one most important trait.

A 2006 survey by a consortium in which SHRM was a participant surveyed over 400 employers across the United States. The employers articulated the skills that new entrants to the workforce need to succeed in the workplace. Among the four most important applied skills across entrants and educational levels were: professionalism/work ethic, oral/written communication, teamwork/collaboration, and critical thinking/problem solving. Unfortunately, entrants across educational levels presented deficiencies in some vital areas. High school graduates were deficient in critical thinking/problem solving based on responses of 69.6% of employers. As for the value of critical thinking/problem solving to the employers, 57% of employers expected this from high school graduates, 72.7% of employers expected this from graduates of two-year higher learning institutions, and 92.1% of employers expected this from graduates of four-year institutions. Unfortunately, only 27.2% of employers rated graduates of four-year institutions with excellent, as opposed to deficient (9%) or adequate (63.5%), critical thinking/problem solving skills.

When interviewed about desirable traits (2010), a scientist at Pearson Talent Assessment stated, "America needs to make sure that our students and our employees are thinking critically, thinking independently, and making judgments" (n.p.). Additionally, a staff member at the American Management Association (n.d.) stated, "Learning leadership and critical thinking skills, along with the traditional skills people learn in school, is a very important tool in terms of building the workforce of tomorrow" (n.p.). A human resources director at Varde (n.d., cited in Pearson Education) further noted, "We really think critical thinking skills are important at any level" and "[i]mproved critical thinking leads to more effective problem solving and improved strategic thinking" (n.p.).

A survey by Hart Research Associates for the American Association of Universities and Colleges (2013) found that 95% of employers surveyed accord hiring preferences to graduates with skills that allow them to contribute to "innovation" in the workplace. These employers noted skills that "cut across majors" as more important than the actual major. In fact, 93% stated, "A candidate's demonstrated capacity to think critically, communicate clearly, and solve complex problems is more important than . . . undergraduate major" (p. 4). Over 75% of employers stated that they wanted academic institutions to place more emphasis on five key learning outcomes for students: critical thinking, complex problem solving, written communication, oral communication, and applied knowledge in real-world settings. Toward this end, employers endorsed several educational practices with the potential to help prepare students for workplace success. These include practices that require students to (a) conduct research and use evidence-based analysis, (b) gain in-depth knowledge in the major and analytic, problem solving, and communication skills, and (c) apply their learning in real-world settings. When asked whether academic institutions should place more, less, or the same as current levels of emphasis on specific learning outcomes, 82% desired more emphasis on critical thinking and analytical reasoning skills; 81% desired more emphasis on the ability to analyze and solve complex problems; 78% wanted more emphasis on the ability to apply knowledge and skills to real-world settings; and 72% wanted more emphasis on the ability to locate, organize, and evaluate information from multiple sources.

Another Hart Research Associates survey for AAUC (2010) revealed employers believe that academic institutions can prepare their graduates for long-term career success with a two-pronged approach, the development of a broad range of skills combined with in-depth skills and knowledge in a specific discipline. Most (89%) employers wanted more emphasis on the ability to communicate effectively (in both oral and written modes), while 81% of employers wanted more emphasis on critical thinking and analytic reasoning skills. Additionally, 75% wanted increased attention to the ability to analyze and solve complex problems, while 68% wanted increased attention to the ability to locate, organize, and evaluate information from multiple sources.

LEAP (Liberal Education and America's Promise) is a national advocacy, campus action, and research initiative that promotes liberal education. The LEAP Campaign (2013) of the AACU is organized around a set of "Essential Learning Outcomes," a statement of what students should gain as they continue into successively higher levels of studies. Included in these outcomes are "Intellectual and Practical Skills," which include inquiry and analysis, critical and creative thinking, written and oral communication, quantitative literacy, information literacy, and teamwork and problem solving. In a Hart Research Associates survey for LEAP (2008), employers graded student learning in college and awarded scores of 8–10 to indicate "well prepared" in an area, 6–7 to indicate "moderately well prepared" in an area, and 1–5 to indicate "not well prepared" in an area. The mean rating for critical thinking was 6.3, with only 22% of respondents awarding it a label of "well prepared." The mean rating for adaptability was 6.3, with only 24% of respondents awarding it a label of "well prepared." CARE (2008) created a resource for project managers in the association and stated, "As a project manager, you will use critical thinking to: understand and use new information; identify, evaluate, and solve problems; and make sound decisions" (n.p.). The resource further stated, "Critical thinking is an essential skill for all aspects of project management . . . The skill helps you organize your thoughts, analyze pros and cons of a situation, and present conclusions in a concise and persuasive manner" (n.p.).

These results collectively indicated that employers in both the public and the private sectors have valued critical thinking as a crucial skill in their staff members and have promoted resources to further develop the application of critical thinking across professional contexts. The need for such efforts across disciplines and professional contexts has continued to be prominent and has necessitated the creation of tools for the evaluation of critical thinking skill.

In the personal realm . . .

Paul (2007), in his address at the 27th Annual International Conference on Critical Thinking, noted, "Critical thinking, if somehow it became generalized in the world, would produce a new and very different world, a world which increasingly is not only in our interest but is necessary to our survival." He further noted, ". . . critical thinking, as I am conceiving it, transforms thinking in two directions. You think more systematically as a result. And you think more comprehensively as a result. And in thinking more comprehensively, you think at a higher level" (n.p.). Brookfield (2012) expanded on this transformation of the world in this observation: "Life is a series of decisions, some small, some much larger. Whom we date or choose as friends, the work or career we pursue, which political candidates we support, what we choose to eat, where we live, what consumer goods we buy, whom we marry and how we raise children – all these decisions are based on assumptions . . . however, the assumptions we base our decisions on have never been examined . . . To make good decisions in life we need to be sure that these assumptions are accurate and valid . . . Critical thinking describes the process we use to uncover and check our assumptions" (n.p.).

© Shutterstock/Login

Gardiner (1998) noted, "Critical thinking is a form of higher-order cognition that society requires and faculty esteem. Many of us believe our society would function far more wisely, harmoniously, and safely in a complex, ever more rapidly changing, and dangerous world if leaders and citizens used critical thinking more consistently than they now do . . ." (p. 123). Mohanan (n.d.) described "general purpose critical thinking" as four related domains, which are (1) the academic domain (e.g., the ability to evaluate the credibility of claims in articles and books written for educated lay readers), (2) the professional domain (e.g., the ability to evaluate options in professional life, such as proposals for company policies), (3) the public domain (e.g., the ability to evaluate ideas and policies, formulate informed opinions, and participate in public matters as responsible citizens), and (4) the private domain (e.g., the ability to evaluate options in private life, such as informed decisions about medical procedures). These and other descriptions of the need for critical thinking in daily life mandate that such skills permeate every area of existence.

Brookfield and other scholars have addressed the value of critical thinking in more recent years. However, the emphasis on thinking has infused the scholarly literature for the past century. In 1910, for instance, Dewey noted, "Thought affords the sole method of escape from purely impulsive or purely routine action" (p. 15). He further noted, "By thought man also develops and arranges artificial signs to remind him in advance of consequences, and of ways of securing and avoiding them" (p. 16), and then concluded, ". . . thought confers upon physical events and objects a very different status and value from that which they possess to a being that does not reflect" (p. 17). Dewey broadened the idea of "education" to encompass any opportunity in which a person can learn, not simply those within the formal school context, and he described the ultimate impact of education on the quality of life: "While it is not the business of education to prove every statement made, any more than to teach every possible item of information, it is its business to cultivate deep-seated and effective habits of discriminating tested beliefs from mere assertions, guesses, and opinions; to develop a lively, sincere, and open-minded preference for conclusions that are properly grounded, and to ingrain into the individual's working habits methods of inquiry and reasoning appropriate to the various problems that present themselves. No matter how much an individual knows as a matter of hearsay and information, if he has not attitudes and habits of this sort, he is not intellectually educated. He lacks the rudiments of mental discipline. And since these habits are not a gift of nature . . . the formation of these habits is the Training of Mind" (p. 28).

Toward the end product of the "training of the mind," the authors of the essay, "On What It Means to Be an Educated Person" (n.n., n.d.) offered seven attributes of the person who participates in critical examination: a balanced mind, an awareness of the relatedness of learning, an awareness of history, an awareness of cultural influence, an awareness of the role of reason, an awareness of the roles of language, and an awareness of moral involvement (p. 2). These authors proposed the ideal of a three-way balance across a basis of humility, an approach of confidence, and a manner of rigor (p. 2). In a modern reiteration of these ideas, Boyer (1995) pondered, "What, then, does it mean to be an educated person? It means respecting the miracle of life, being empowered in the use of language, and responding sensitively to the aesthetic. Being truly educated means putting learning in historical perspective, understanding groups and institutions, having reverence for the natural world, and affirming the dignity of work. And, above all, being an educated person means being guided by values and beliefs and connecting the lessons of the classroom to the realities of life" (n.p.).

In response to the question, "How has critical thinking changed your life?" Chaffee (1993) said, "Critical thinking IS my life; it's my philosophy of life. It's how I define myself . . . I'm an educator because I think these ideas have meaning. I'm convinced that what we believe in has to be able to stand the test of evaluation" (p. 44). Facione (2006), on the topic of what critical thinking is and why it is so important, presented statements with which a person would agree or disagree based upon whether he or she was disposed toward critical thinking. For instance, an individual disposed toward critical thinking would probably agree with statements like, "I hate talk shows where people shout their opinions but never give any reasons at all," and "I hold off making decisions until I've thought through my options" (p. 10). Conversely, an individual weakly disposed toward critical thinking would probably agree with statements like, "I prefer jobs where the supervisor says exactly what to do and exactly how to do it," and "I hate when teachers discuss problems instead of just giving the answers" (p. 10).

Like Boyer, Facione (2006) noted the influence on life and living of critical thinking, then enumerated varied traits of the critical thinker: inquisitiveness with regard to a wide range of issues; concern to become and remain well informed; alertness to opportunities to use critical thinking; trust in the processes of reasoned inquiry; self-confidence in one's own abilities to reason; open-mindedness regarding divergent worldviews; flexibility in considering alternatives and opinions; understanding of the opinions of other people; fair-mindedness in appraising reasoning; honesty in facing one's own biases, prejudices, stereotypes, or egocentric tendencies; prudence in suspending, making or altering judgments; and willingness to reconsider and revise views where honest reflection suggests that change is warranted (p. 9). In his widely known essay, "Critical Thinking: What It Is and Why It Counts," Facione (2006) summarized the value of critical thinking as this: "Teach people to make good decisions and you equip them to improve their own futures and become contributing members of society, rather than burdens on society. Becoming educated and practicing good judgment does not absolutely guarantee a life of happiness, virtue, or economic success, but it surely offers a better chance at those things. And it is clearly better than enduring the consequences of making bad decisions and better than burdening friends, family, and all the rest of us with the unwanted and avoidable consequences of those poor choices" (n.p.). Finally, Schick and Vaughn (2013) noted, "You hear a lot of 'whats,' but seldom any good 'whys.' You hear the beliefs, but seldom any solid reasons behind them - nothing substantial enough to indicate that these assertions are likely to be true. You may hear naiveté, passionate advocacy, fierce denunciation, one-sided sifting of evidence, defense of the party line, leaps of faith, jumps to false conclusions, plunges into wishful thinking, and courageous stands on the shaky ground of subjective certainty. But the good reasons are missing.

Without good 'whys' our beliefs are simply arbitrary, with no more claim to knowledge than the random choice of a playing card. Without good 'whys' to guide us, our beliefs lose their value in a world where beliefs are already a dime a dozen" (p. 2).

© Shutterstock/Red_Spruce

Conclusion

In this section, we have overviewed the need for critical thinking as demonstrated by academic institutions, professional associations, work sites and work duties, and the circumstances of day-to-day life. We believe that the quantity and quality of the evidence we have presented underscore the need for evaluation and enhancement of critical thinking across a variety of contexts, including the continuum of professional development for SLPs.

References

ABIM Foundation. (2002). Medical professionalism in the new millennium: A physician charter. Annals of Internal Medicine, 136(3), 263-246.

Albuquerque Public Schools. (2007). F Mission statement. Available from http://www.aps.edu/about-us/policies-and-procedural-directives/policies/a.-foundations-and-basic-commitments/a.01-mission-statement. Retrieved 10/01/2014.

American Association of Colleges and Universities. (2013). Project LEAP. Available from https://www.aacu.org/leap. Retrieved 10/01/2014.

American Dental Association. (n.d.). Principles of ethics and code of professional conduct. Chicago, IL: American Dental Association. Available from http://www.ada.org/en/about-the-ada/principles-of-ethics-code-of-professional-conduct. Retrieved 10/01/2014.

American Medical Association. (2001). Principles of medical ethics. Chicago, IL: American Medical Association. Available from http://www.ama-assn.org/ama/pub/physician-resources/medical-ethics/code-medical-ethics.page. Retrieved 10/01/2014.

American Nursing Association. (2001). Professional standards, policy, and practice. Silver Spring, MD: American Nursing Association. Available from http://www.nursingworld.org/Mobile/Code-of-Ethics. Retrieved 10/01/2014.

American Occupational Therapy Association. (2010). Occupational therapy code of ethics and ethics standards. Bethesda, MD: American Occupational Therapy Association. Available from https://www.aota.org/-/media/Corporate/Files/AboutAOTA/OfficialDocs/Ethics/Code%20and%20Ethics%20Standards%202010.pdf. Retrieved 10/01/2014.

American Physical Therapy Association. (n.d.). Code of ethics for the physical therapist. Alexandria, VA: American Physical Therapy Association. Available from http://www.apta.org/search.aspx?q=code%20of%20ethics. Retrieved 10/0120/14.

American Psychological Association. (2002). Ethical principles of psychologists and code of conduct. Washington, DC: American Psychological Association. Available from http://www.apa.org/ethics/code/index.aspx. Retrieved 10/01/2014.

American Speech-Language-Hearing Association. (2010r). Code of ethics [Ethics]. Available from www.asha.org/policy. Retrieved 10/01/2014.

Arum, R., & Roksa, J. (2011). Academically adrift: Limited learning on college campuses. Chicago, IL: University of Chicago Press.

Arum, R., Roksa, J., & Cho, E. (2010). Improving undergraduate learning: Findings and policy recommendations from the SSRC-CLA Longitudinal Project. Brooklyn, NY: Social Science Research Council.

Astin, A. W. (1991). Assessment for excellence: The philosophy and practice of assessment and evaluation in Higher Education. New York, NY: MacMillan Publishing.

Barr, R., & Tagg, J. (1995). From teaching to learning: A new paradigm for undergraduate education. Change: The Magazine of Higher Learning, 27(6), 12-25.

Bell, S. K., Delbanco, T., Anderson-Shaw, L., McDonald, T. B., & Gallagher, T. H. (2011). Accountability for medical error: Moving beyond blame to advocacy. Chest, 140(2), 519-526.

Bismarck Public Schools (2010). Parent-student handbook 2010-2012. Bismarck, ND: Bismarck Public Schools.

Boyer, E. (1995). The educated person. In ASCD 1995 Yearbook, p. 16. Alexandria, VA: Association for Supervision and Curriculum Development.

Brinkerhood, D. (2003). Accountability and health systems: Overview, framework, and strategies. Bethesda, MD: ABT Associates, Partners for Health Reform.

Brookfield, S. (2012). Developing critical thinkers. Seminar presented to Teachers' College, Columbia University, New York, NY.

Cascade Canyon School. (n.d.). Mission statement. Available from http://www.privateschoolreview.com/school_ov/school_id/1619. Retrieved 10/01/2014.

Cascia Hall Preparatory School. (2014). 2014-2015 student handbook. Tulsa, OK: Cascia Hall Preparatory School.

Chaffee, J. (1993). Critical thinking. In J. Esterle and D. Cluman (Eds.), Conversations with critical thinkers. San Francisco, CA: Whitman Institute.

Collegiate School, The. (n.d.). Mission statement. Available from http://www.collegiate-va.org/Page/About/Welcome. Retrieved 10/01/2014.

Colorado Academy, The. (n.d.). Mission statement. Available from http://www.coloradoacademy.org/page/About/About-CA. Retrieved 10/01/2014.

Cooperative for Assistance and Relief Everywhere, Inc. (CARE). (2008). Key resources for project managers: Critical thinking. Atlanta, GA: CARE, Inc.

Council for Aid to Education. (2006). Collegiate learning assessment. New York, NY: Council for Aid to Education.

Cronon, W. (1998). The goals of a liberal education. The American Scholar, 67(4), 73-80.

Cuban, L. (2010). A democracy needs diverse good schools, not one-size-fits-all. Available from http://larrycuban.wordpress.com/2010/06/02/a-democracy-needs-diverse-good-schools-not-one-size-fits-all/. Retrieved 10/01/2014.

Denver Public Schools. (n.d.). Mission statement. Available from https://www.dpsk12.org/policies/. Retrieved 10/01/2014.

Dewey, J. (1910). How we think. Chicago, IL: D. C. Heath & Company Publishers.

Donaldson, L. (2001). Professional accountability in a changing world. Postgraduate Medical Journal, 77, 65-67.

Emanuel, E. J., & Emanuel, L. L. (1996). What is accountability in health care? Annals of Internal Medicine, 124, 229-239.

Epstein, R. M., & Hundert, E. M. (2002). Defining and assessing professional competence. Journal of the American Medical Association, 287(2), 226-235.

Facione, P. A. (2006). Critical thinking: What it is and why it counts. San Jose, CA: Insight Assessment.

Family School, The. (n.d.). Mission statement. Available from http://www.privateschoolreview.com/school_ov/school_id/4393. Retrieved 10/01/2014.

Gambrill, E. (1999). Evidence-based practice: An alternative to authority-based practice. Families in Society: The Journal of Contemporary Social Services, 80(4), 341-350.

Gambrill, E. (2004). Contributions of critical thinking and evidence-based practice to the fulfillment of the ethical obligations of professionals. In H. E. Briggs and T. L. Rzepnicki (Eds.), Using evidence in social work practice: Behavioral perspectives. (pp. 3-19). Chicago, IL: Lyceum Books.

Gardiner, L. (1998). Why we must change: The research evidence. The NEA Higher Education Journal, 121-138.
Gatto, J. T. (2009). The curriculum of necessity or what must an educated person know? Available from http://www.missionislam.com/homed/neseducation.htm Retrieved 10/01/2014.
Giancarlo, C. A., & Facione, P. A. (2001). A look across four years at the disposition toward critical thinking among undergraduate students. The Journal of General Education, 50(1), 29-55.
Groton Public Schools. (n.d.). District vision. Available from http://www.groton.k12.ct.us/Page/110. Retrieved 10/01/2014.
Hart Research Associates. (2008). How should colleges assess and improve student learning? Employers views on the accountability challenge. Washington, DC: Peter D. Hart Research Associates.
Hart Research Associates. (2010). Raising the bar: Employers' views on college learning in the wake of the economic downturn. Washington, DC: Peter D. Hart Research Associates.
Hart Research Associates. (2013). It takes more than a major: Employer priorities for college learning and student success. Washington, DC: Peter D. Hart Research Associates.
Harvard College. (n.d.). Undergraduate mission statement. Available from http://www.harvard.edu/faqs/mission-statement. Retrieved 10/01/2014.
Hume-Fogg Magnet High School. (n.d.). Mission statement. Available from http://humefogghs.mnps.org/pages/Hume_Fogg_Magnet_High_School. Retrieved 10/01/2014.
Iowa State University. (2014). Mission statement. Available from http://catalog.iastate.edu/. Retrieved 10/01/2014.
Kaufman, J. (2011). What must an educated person know? Available from http://www.informationliberation.com/?id=27324. Retrieved 10/01/2014.
Kurfiss, J. (1988). Critical thinking: Theory, research, practice, and possibilities. ASHE-ERIC Higher Education Report No. 2. Washington, DC: Association for the Study of Higher Education.
Lampert, N. (2007). Critical thinking dispositions as an outcome of undergraduate education. The Journal of General Education, 56(1), 17-33.
Lawrenceville School, The. (n.d.). Mission statement. Available from http://www.lawrenceville.org/about/our-mission/index.aspx. Retrieved 10/01/2014.
Leonard, M. W., & Frankel, A. (2010). The path to safe and reliable healthcare. Patient Education and Counseling, 80, 288-292.
Ley, P. (1988). Communicating with patients: Improving communication, satisfaction, and compliance. New York, NY: Croom-Helm Publishers.
Manion, J. (2011). From management to leadership: Strategies for transforming health care. San Francisco, CA: Jossey-Bass Publishers.
Maudsley, G., & Strivens, J. (2001). 'Science', 'critical thinking', and 'competence' for tomorrow's doctors: A review of terms and concepts. Medical Education, 34(1), 53-60.
Mayhew, R. (n.d.). Examples of using critical thinking to make decisions in the workplace. Available from http://smallbusiness.chron.com/examples-using-critical-thinking-make-decisions-workplace-12952.html. Retrieved 10/01/2014.
McGregor, T. (2010). Characteristics of an educated person. Available from http://hubpages.com/hub/Chracteristics-of-an-educated-person. Retrieved 10/01/2014.
Mead, R. (2010, June 7). Learning by degrees. New Yorker Magazine.
Mind Tools. (n.d.). Building good work relationships: Making work enjoyable and productive. Available from http://www.mindtools.com/pages/article/good-relationships.htm. Retrieved 10/01/2014.
Mohanan, K. P. (2005). Who is an educated person? Ingredients of educatedness. Centre for Development of Teaching and Learning. National University of Singapore. Available from http://www.iiserpune.ac.in/~mohanan/educated/default.htm. Retrieved 10/01/2014.
Mohanan, K. P. (n.d.). What is critical thinking? Centre for Development of Teaching and Learning, National University of Singapore. Available from http://www.cdtl.nus.edu.sg/ctp/critical.htm. Retrieved 10/01/2014.
National Association of Social Workers. (2008). Code of ethics. Washington, DC: National Association of Social Workers. Available from http://www.naswdc.org/pubs/code/default.asp. Retrieved 10/01/2014.
National Education Association. (1975). Code of ethics. Washington, DC: National Education Association. Available from http://www.nea.org/home/30442.htm. Retrieved 10/01/2014.
Northwestern University. (n.d.). Mission statement. Available from http://www.northwestern.edu/provost/about/. Retrieved 10/01/2014.

O'Hagan, J., & Persaud, D. (2009). Creating a culture of accountability in health care. The Health Care Manager, 28, 124-133.
On what it means to be an educated person. (n.d.). Available from https://www.umassd.edu/media/umassdartmouth/fycm/whatitmeansedpers.pdf. Retrieved 10/01/2014.
Oxford Academy, The. (n.d.). Mission statement. Available from http://oxford.auhsd.us/Oxford/6090-General-Information.html. Retrieved 10/01/2014.
Paul, R. (2004). The state of critical thinking today. Tomales, CA: The Critical Thinking Community.
Paul, R. (2007). Critical thinking in every domain of knowledge and belief. Keynote Address, 27th Annual International Conference on Critical Thinking, Berkeley, CA.
Paul, R., Elder, L., & Bartell, T. (1997). California teacher preparation for instruction in critical thinking: Research findings and policy recommendations. Sacramento, CA: California Commission on Teacher Credentialing.
Pearson Education. (n.d.). Critical thinking seen as today's number one skill. Available from http://www.pearsoned.com/critical-thinking-seen-as-todays-number-one-skill/#.VKS4livF8_8. Retrieved 10/01/2014.
Pearson Education. (n.d.). Pearson talent assessment. Upper Saddle River, NJ: Pearson Education.
Pennsylvania State System of Higher Education. (n.d.). 2020 Strategic Plan. Available from http://www.passhe.edu/inside/bog/Documents/Strategic%20Plan%202020%20Rising%20to%20the%20Challenge_10-14.pdf. Retrieved 10/01/2014.
Perie, M., Grigg, W. S., & Donahue, P. L. (2005). The nation's report card: Reading 2005 (NCES 2006–451). U.S. Department of Education, Institute of Education Sciences, National Center for Education Statistics. Washington, DC: U.S. Government Printing Office.
Robinson, G. (2002). Effective doctor patient communication: Building bridges and bridging barriers. Canadian Journal of Neurological Science, 29, 30-32.
Roeper School, The. (2008). Mission statement. Available from http://www.roeper.org/Mission-Statement. Retrieved 10/01/2014.
Salem Public Schools. (2013). Mission statement. Available from http://salem.k12.ma.us/pages/SPS_DistWebDocs/District_Mission_Statement.pdf. Retrieved 10/01/2014.
Schick, T., & Vaughn, L. (2013). How to think about weird things: Critical thinking for a new age (7th ed.). Columbus, OH: McGraw-Hill Publishers.
Seymour, B., Kinn, S., & Sutherland, N. (2003). Valuing both critical and creative thinking in clinical practice: Narrowing the research-practice gap. Journal of Advanced Nursing, 42(3), 288-296.
Society for Human Resource Management. (2006). Are they really ready to work? Employers' perspectives on the basic knowledge and applied skills of new entrants to the 21st century workforce. Alexandria, VA: Society for Human Resource Management.
Society for Human Resource Management. (2014). Technology survey findings: Recruitment for business and IT employment opportunities. Alexandria, VA: Society for Human Resource Management.
Sparks, D. (2010). What it means to be an educated person. Available from http://www.annarbor.com/news/education/what-it-means-to-be-an-educated-person/ Retrieved 10/01/2014.
Stanton College Preparatory School. (n.d.). Mission statement. Available from http://www.stantoncollegeprep.org/central/?q=node/28. Retrieved 10/01/2014.
Tang, P. C., & Newcomb, C. (1998). Informing patients: a guide for providing patient health information. *Journal of the American Medical Informatics Association*, 5(6), 563-570.
Topeka Public Schools. (n.d.). Guiding documents. Available from http://www.topekapublicschools.net/guiding/. Retrieved 10/01/2014.
University of California, The. (n.d.). Mission statement. Available from http://accreditation.ucmerced.edu/files/public/documents/Portfolio/Exhibits/Exhibits_S1/1.1. Retrieved 10/01/2014.
University of Chicago Laboratory Schools, The. (n.d.). Mission statement. Available from http://www.ucls.uchicago.edu/about-lab/mission-statement/index.aspx. Retrieved 10/01/2014.
University of Denver, The. (n.d.). University vision, mission, values, and goals. Available from http://www.du.edu/chancellor/vision/. Retrieved 10/01/2014.
University of Kansas, The. (n.d.). Mission statement. Available from http://www.ku.edu/about/mission/. Retrieved 10/01/2014.
University of Portland, The. (n.d.). Mission statement. Available from http://www.up.edu/about/default.aspx?cid=8263. Retrieved 10/01/2014.

University School, The. (n.d.). Mission statement. Available from http://www.usn.org/page/Curriculum/The-High-School/Introduction-to-the-High-School. Retrieved 10/01/2014.

University of Tennessee, The. (n.d.). Vision statement. Available from http://www.utk.edu/aboutut/vision/. Retrieved 10/01/2014.

Van Nuys High School. (n.d.). Mission statement. Available from http://www.edline.net/pages/Van_Nuys_Senior_High/School_Info/Mission_Statement. Retrieved 10/01/2014.

Vratny, A., & Shriver, D. (2007). A conceptual model for growing evidence-based practice. Nursing Administration Quarterly, 31(2), 162-170.

Wachter, R. (2012). Personal accountability in healthcare: Searching for the right balance. London, UK: The Health Foundation.

Wake Forest University. (n.d.). Vision and mission statements. Available from http://strategicplan.wfu.edu/vision.mission.html. Retrieved 10/01/2014.

William Penn Charter School. (n.d.). Vision, mission, and philosophy. Available from http://www.penncharter.com/page.cfm?p=2022. Retrieved 10/01/2014.

Yanklowitz, S. (2013). A society with poor critical thinking skills: The case for 'argument' in education. Available from http://www.huffingtonpost.com. Retrieved 10/01/2014.

part 2

THE DEFINITIONS AND DESCRIPTIONS OF CRITICAL THINKING

In Part 1, we overviewed the mandate for critical thinking from a myriad of sources. The term "critical thinking" was ubiquitous within these mandates. But what actually is critical thinking? Whom would we describe as a critical thinker? And what characteristics would a critical thinker exhibit? In Part 2, we describe various approaches to the definition and description of critical thinking.

Definition of Critical Thinking

Sanders and Moulenbelt (2011) posited, "there appears to be no widely accepted definition of critical thinking" (p. 38). They noted that, while this is troublesome, the fact that academicians assert that their definitions are normative is also troublesome. They overviewed a collection of definitions of critical thinking and characterized them as either "context specific" (i.e., influenced by the tenets of a particular academic discipline) or "cross-disciplinary" (i.e., comprised of principles that transcend disciplinary boundaries).

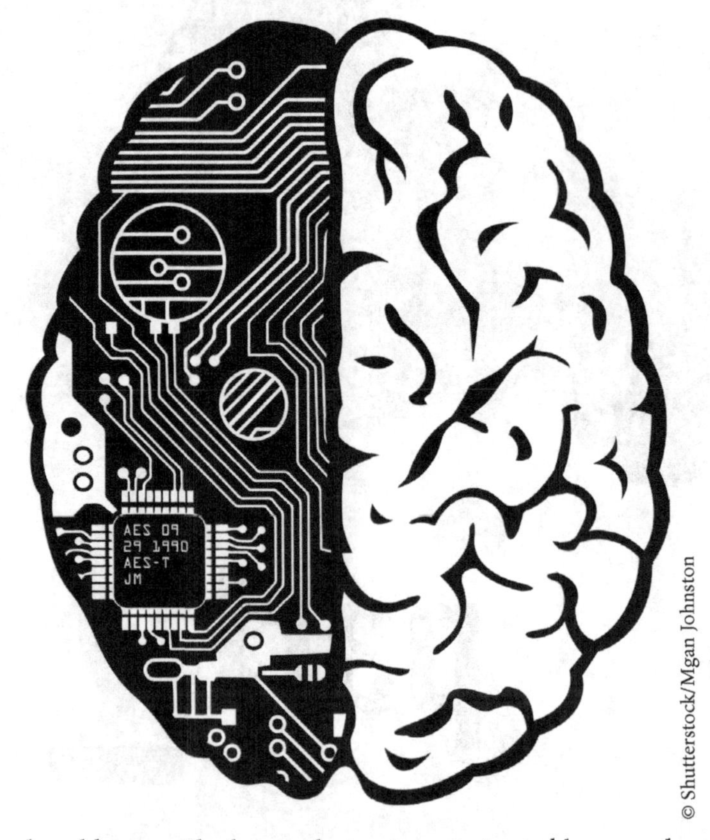

© Shutterstock/Mgan Johnston

They then noted that, because of the lack of a uniform definition, assessment of critical thinking—a current focus of assessment at the university level—becomes problematic. Bailin, Case, Coombs, and Daniels (1999) echoed the sentiments of Sanders and Moulenbelt in their observation: "Given the vagueness of the concept of critical thinking and the variety of ways critical thinking competence can be described, it would be foolish to suggest that any given conception of critical thinking is *the* correct one. It does not follow from this, however, that all conceptions of critical thinking are equally good or defensible" (p. 285). Garrison (1991) further explained the problem as he noted, "One of the major difficulties with understanding critical thinking in an educational context is the fragmentation of conceptualizing the thinking process itself. At various times authors have associated critical thinking with problem solving but not creative thinking; with deductive but not inductive thinking; with ill-defined but not well-defined problems; with abstract but not concrete problems; and with relevance but not rigor" (p. 287).

Taken as a whole, these observations document the diversity and, in some cases, incongruity across definitions of critical thinking. To illustrate this diversity, we have included a sample of the available definitions of critical thinking within the psychology, education, philosophy, and related literature.

Some of the definitions from the literature are capsule definitions, expressed in one to two sentences.

From Lipman (1988):

"Critical thinking is thinking that both employs criteria and can be assessed by appeal to criteria" (p. 38).

From The American Philosophical Association (Facione, 1990):

Critical thinking is "the process of purposeful, self-regulatory judgment. The process gives reasoned consideration to evidence, contexts, conceptualizations, methods, and criteria" (p. 2).

From Halonen (1996):

"(Critical thinking is) the propensity and skills to engage in activity with reflective skepticism focused on deciding what to believe or do" (p. 6).

From Moon (2005):

"Critical thinking is a capacity to work with complex ideas whereby a person can make effective provision of evidence to justify a reasonable judgment. The evidence, and therefore the judgment, will pay appropriate attention to context" (p. 7).

From Saiz and Rivas (2008):

"Critical thinking is a process of seeking knowledge, through reasoning skills, the solution to problems, and decision making, affording us – with greater efficacy – the desired results" (p. 26).

© Shutterstock/graphixmania

From Mulnix (2012):

"(Critical thinking) . . . fundamentally consists in acquiring, developing, and exercising the ability to grasp inferential connections holding between statements" (p. 464).

From Nordquist (n.d.):

Critical thinking is, "The process of independently analyzing, synthesizing, and evaluating information as a guide to behavior and beliefs" (n.p.).

From Haskins (2013):

Critical thinking is, "A process by which we use our knowledge and intelligence to effectively arrive at the most reasonable and justifiable positions on issues, and which endeavors to identify and overcome the numerous hindrances to rational thinking" (n.p.).

Some of the definitions from the literature are more extensive definitions that contain descriptions of the dispositions and/or processes associated with critical thinking.

From Glaser (1941):

"... Critical thinking calls for a persistent effort to examine any belief or supposed form of knowledge in the light of the evidence that supports it and the further conclusions to which it tends. It also generally requires ability to recognize problems, to find workable means for meeting those problems, to gather and marshal pertinent information, to recognize unstated assumptions and values, to comprehend and use language with accuracy, clarity, and discrimination, to interpret data, to appraise evidence and evaluate arguments, to recognize the existence (or non-existence) of logical relationships between propositions, to draw warranted conclusions and generalizations, to put to test the conclusions and generalizations at which one arrives, to reconstruct one's patterns of beliefs on the basis of wider experience and to render accurate judgments about specific things and qualities in everyday life" (p. 6).

From Scriven and Paul (1987):

"Critical thinking is the intellectually disciplined process of actively and skillfully conceptualizing, applying, analyzing, synthesizing, and/or evaluating information gathered from, or generated by, observation, experience, reflection, reasoning, or communication, as a guide to belief and action. In its exemplary form, it is based on universal intellectual values that transcend subject matter divisions: clarity, accuracy, precision, consistency, relevance, sound evidence, good reasons, depth, breadth, and fairness" (n.p.).

From the National Council for Excellence in Critical Thinking (1987):

"(Critical thinking) entails the examination of those structures or elements of thought implicit in all reasoning: purpose, problem, or question-at-issue; assumptions; concepts; empirical grounding; reasoning leading to conclusions; implications and consequences; objections from alternative viewpoints; and frame of reference. Critical thinking — in being responsive to variable subject matter, issues, and purposes — is incorporated in a family of interwoven modes of thinking, among them: scientific thinking, mathematical thinking, historical thinking, anthropological thinking, economic thinking, moral thinking, and philosophical thinking" (n.p.).

From Elder (2007):

"Critical thinking is self-guided, self-disciplined thinking which attempts to reason at the highest level of quality in a fair-minded way. People who think critically consistently attempt to live rationally, reasonably, (and) empathically . . . They use the intellectual tools that critical thinking offers - concepts and principles that enable them to analyze, assess, and improve thinking. They work diligently to develop the intellectual virtues of intellectual integrity, intellectual humility, intellectual civility, intellectual empathy, intellectual sense of justice and confidence in reason" (n.p.).

From Paul and Elder (2008):

"Critical thinking is that mode of thinking - about any subject, content, or problem - in which the thinker improves the quality of his or her thinking by skillfully taking charge of the structures inherent in thinking and imposing intellectual standards upon them . . . Critical thinking is, in short, self-directed, self-disciplined, self-monitored, and self-corrective thinking. It presupposes assent to rigorous standards of excellence and mindful command of their use. It entails effective communication and problem solving abilities and a commitment to overcome our native egocentrism and sociocentrism" (p. 4).

From the Education Portal (n.d.):

"Critical thinking means making reasoned judgments that are logical and well thought out. It is a way of thinking in which you don't simply accept all arguments and conclusions you are exposed to but rather have an attitude involving questioning such arguments and conclusions. It requires wanting to see what evidence is involved to support a particular argument or conclusion. People who use critical thinking are the ones who say things such as, 'How do you know that? Is this conclusion based on evidence or gut feelings?' and 'Are there alternative possibilities?' when given new pieces of information" (n.p.).

From Halpern, Stephenson, and Williams (2009):

Critical thinking is "the use of those cognitive skills or strategies that increase the probability of a desirable outcome. It is purposeful, reasoned, and goal-directed. It is the kind of thinking involved in solving problems, formulating inferences, calculating likelihoods, and making decisions. When people think critically, they are evaluating the outcomes of their thought processes—how good a decision is or how well a problem is solved. Critical thinking also involves evaluating the thinking process—the reasoning that went into the conclusion arrived at or the kinds of factors considered in making a decision" (n.p.).

From Halpern (2014):

"Critical thinking is the use of those cognitive skills or strategies that increase the probability of a desirable outcome. It is used to describe thinking that is purposeful, reasoned, and goal directed—the kind of thinking involved in solving problems, formulating inferences, calculating likelihoods, and making decisions, when the thinker is using skills that are thoughtful and effective for the particular context and type of thinking task" (p. 7).

With such a variety of definitions available that resemble each other in many instances, scholars have questioned whether themes exist across these definitions regardless of the orientation reflected in particular definitions. Moore (2011) explored the ideas that academicians in three disciplines—history, philosophy, cultural studies—held about the nature of critical thinking. He identified at least seven definitional strands for critical thinking in the commentaries of his research participants: (1) as judgment, (2) as skepticism, (3) as simple originality, (4) as sensitive reading, (5) as rationality, (6) as activist engagement with knowledge, and (7) as self-reflexivity. Then, in 2014, Geng conducted a content analysis of the definition of critical thinking. His review of 64 definitions provided by scholars across a variety of disciplines revealed some common perceived characteristics of critical thinkers: judgment, argument, questioning, information processing, problem solving, metacognition, and critical thinking disposition. He also noted that the disciplinary backgrounds of scholars directly influence their approaches to conceptualization of critical thinking. With this in mind, we now present an overview of models, which contain not only definitions but also descriptions of concepts and processes of critical thinking, available in the literature to further explore the nature of critical thinking.

Models of Critical Thinking

A model of a phenomenon is an explanation of that phenomenon. A model of critical thinking, then, is an explanation of one or more aspects of critical thinking. A model may attempt to isolate the skills inherent in critical thinking, then describe the relative value of each of these skills for the critical thinking process. Or, a model may attempt to describe the characteristics of individuals who have demonstrated effective critical thinking in an attempt to specify the personal characteristics that are correlated with this critical thinking process. A model may attempt to outline the development in the sophistication of critical thinking, then document the specific milestones that an individual attains in the course of the maturation of the critical thinking process. Or, a model may relate critical thinking to other processes involved in learning and interacting with knowledge. As noted in the presentation of examples of definitions of critical thinking, no authoritative consensus exists as to how to conceptualize this phenomenon (or collection of phenomena, as the case may be). However, several scholars have created models of critical thinking in their attempts to organize sometimes disparate information into a unified explanation. We now move into an

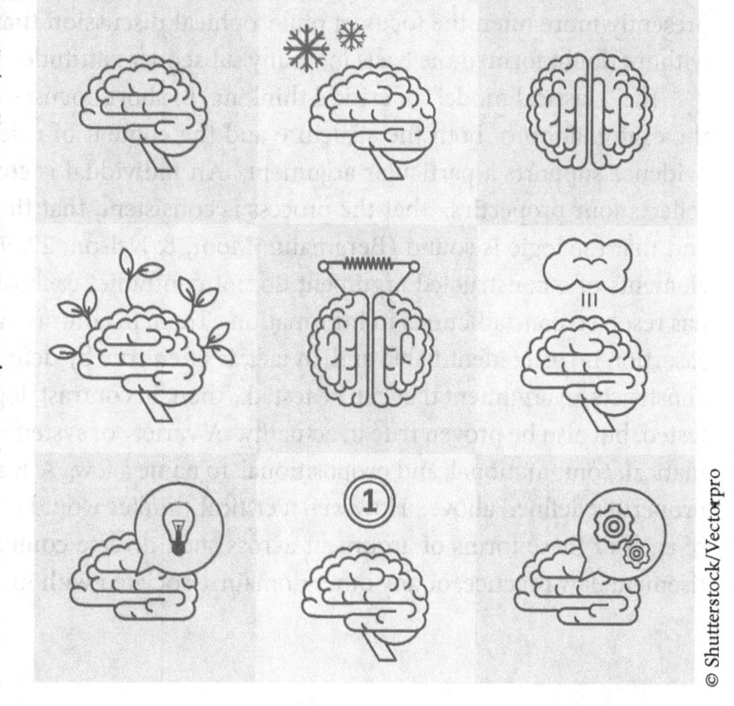

overview of the primary models available in the literature, with a summary of the primary tenets of each explanation.

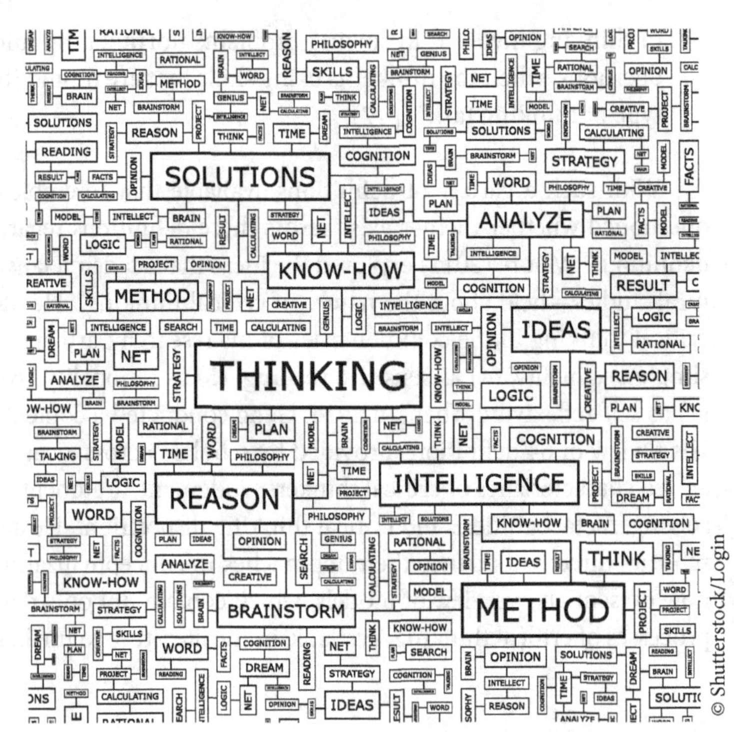

© Shutterstock/Login

Classical Model

In his classic reflection on the beginning of critical thinking, James Harvey Robinson (1921) characterized classical civilizations, such as the Mesopotamian civilization, as primitive in their beliefs in that they accepted certain information without question. He noted, however, that as time moved forward the desire to question also moved forward and that classical civilizations, such as the Greek civilization, developed systematic ways, beginning with the preservation and dissemination of ideas in written forms (i.e., books), to advance the expansion of the mind. Robinson noted that, in the absence of what he called the "venerated classics," individuals came to hold suspect the "simple, spontaneous, and ancient ways of looking at things" (p. 9). This freedom to suspect led to the appearance of those whose mode of operation was doubt—that is, doubt which led to questions, which (was the hope, at least) led to the truth. In addition to the dissemination of ideas in written form, the Greek thinkers promoted the concept of metaphysics, which Robinson noted "busies itself with conceptions, abstractions, distinctions, hypotheses, postulates, and logical inferences" (p. 10). While classical ideas are presently more often the focus of philosophical discussion than of conscious application, these ideas have without doubt formed the basis for many subsequent attitudes toward critical thinking.

The "classical model" of critical thinking, in short, focuses on the development of logic. Logic involves the examination of both the structure and the content of evidence to determine whether the sum of the evidence supports a particular argument. An individual is considered "logical" when his or her thinking reflects four properties: that the process is consistent, that the process is valid, that the logic is complete, and that the logic is sound (Bergmann, Moor, & Nelson, 2009). A consistent process is one in which the elements of a constructed argument do not contradict each other, which often reflects that an individual has resolved contradictions in information. Then, in contrast, a valid process is one in which what is a true assertion is easily identifiable and, in fact, is often true by definition. Logic is complete when an individual constructs an argument that can be tested. Then, in contrast, logic is sound when not only can arguments be tested, but also be proven true in actuality. A variety of systems of logic exist, such as philosophical, mathematical, computational, and propositional, to name a few. A system need not directly reflect each of the four properties defined above. However, a critical thinker would at some point demonstrate his or her mastery of each of these forms of argument across such diverse contexts as debate, experimental research, advertisement, law practice, or any other domain associated with his or her academic or professional discipline.

Scientific Method Model

© Shutterstock/ PlusONE

Another model views critical thinking as the application of the scientific method. While the term "scientific method" stimulates images of scientists in their laboratories surrounded by their beakers, petri dishes, telescopes, lasers, or other equipment, in actuality an individual need not be in a lab (or even be a scientist, per se) to still apply this method of thinking to answering questions and solving problems across situations that arise on a day-to-day basis.

The "scientific method" involves a rational order of steps that allow scientists to reach conclusions about the world. Application of the scientific method starts with the formulation of a question. This question typically arises after an exploration of the relevant literature and/or the observation of a specific phenomenon. The question may take the form of a hypothesis, or a prediction that research will yield a specific result. At this point, the scientific method involves the creation of a systematic way to collect information to test this hypothesis. This is known as the design phase and may utilize one of a number of available experimental designs. Strict adherence to the procedures mandated by a particular design will result in the collection of the most valid data. At this point, the scientific method involves the analysis and interpretation of these data and then the formulation of a conclusion as to whether the data support the hypothesis. Ultimately, application of the scientific method will allow an individual to explore a phenomenon, discover new knowledge, expand or correct previous knowledge, or integrate previous knowledge.

Skills Model

Another approach to conceptualization of critical thinking focuses upon the identification of skills that are relevant to the critical thinking process. These models presume that, if an individual possesses this set of skills, he or she will then be successful in various critical thinking tasks. We now overview representative "skills models" whose creators have attempted to delineate the capabilities that are essential to critical thinking.

Model #1: Haskins

Haskins (2013) described a five-step model of critical thinking that delineated specific skills that a critical thinker has at each step of the critical thinking process. He noted that the critical thinker was not one predisposed to find flaws but rather was one who remained neutral and unbiased in the critical process. He also noted that, because of their individual values and principles, those considered critical thinkers did not necessarily reach the same conclusions at the end of this process. Their commonality was that they followed a systematic plan to evaluate claims and opinions. A brief description of each step in his conceptualization of this process follows:

© Shutterstock/rassco

Step 1: Adoption of the Attitude of a Critical Thinker

Haskins asserted that the proper attitude for a critical thinker reflects a number of traits. The partnership of open mindedness paired with a healthy skepticism results in a critical thinker who is neither dogmatic nor gullible. This leads to seeking out facts from various information sources, then using reasoning to judge issues. This also involves exploring issues from as many sides as possible while critiquing both the pros and the cons for each side examined. The attitude of intellectual humility serves as a reminder to a critical thinker that he or she may be in error and that the search for truth—rather than the attempt to please others or to criticize their views—is the appropriate aim. Humility also leads one to admit that he or she may not know, at least to a stated degree of certainty, and to realize that most issues have a certain degree of complexity. The attitude of intellectual independence serves as a reminder that, while the motivation to conform is powerful, one must reject conformity in favor of objective evaluation of evidence. And, as for motivation, he noted that a critical thinker must be motivated to invest the necessary work to sufficiently evaluate multiple sides of issues—work that involves rejection of intellectual laziness.

Step 2: Recognition, then Avoidance, of Hindrances to Critical Thinking

Haskins differentiated unintentional hindrances (e.g., natural human limitations) from intentional hindrances to critical thinking, which can be subtle or even insidious and involve faulty use of language, faulty use of logic, and psychological and sociological issues. With respect to unintentional hindrances, Haskins noted that, as humans, we are not perfect and thus may not see the world with total objectivity and clarity because of faults in facts, perceptions, memories, and biases. Because of that, the best for which a critical thinker may hope is comprehension of an issue—comprehension that, while not perfect, is sufficient as the starting point for the process of critical thinking. Examples of natural human limitations include false memories, confirmation biases, perception limitations, personal biases, physical or emotional hindrances, and reliance primarily on testimonial evidence. Examples of language-based limitations include value accorded to expressions that assure, doublespeak terms, emotive content, and meaningless comparisons, while examples of logic-based limitations include reliance on superstitions, use of false analogies, reliance on irrelevant comparisons, use of non sequitur arguments, and reliance on quantities rather than qualities of populations. Wishful thinking, self-deceiving, censoring, shoehorning, and conforming also hinder critical thinking.

Step 3: Identification and Characterization of Arguments

Haskins acknowledged the negative connotations of the word "argument" and indicated that, in the process of critical thinking, the word does not mean to quarrel or complain. Instead, an argument involves the presentation of a reason(s) to support a conclusion(s), with at least one reason statement and at least one conclusion statement necessary for every argument. He provided synonyms for both reasons (e.g., data, propositions, evidence, verifications) and conclusions (e.g., claims, verdicts, actions, opinions). He further divided arguments into those that are deductive—from a general conclusion to a specific application—and those that are inductive—from specific applications to a general conclusion. Such reflection on the nature of arguments is central to critical thinking.

Step 4: Evaluation of Sources of Information

Given that arguments incorporate information, fallacious information by definition leads to fallacious arguments. Because of this, Haskins provided four questions that a critical thinker should ask about the sources of information to determine whether those sources are credible, unbiased, and accurate: (1) Does the information source have the necessary qualifications or level of comprehension to make a claim? (2) Does the source have a reputation for accuracy? (3) Does the source have a reason to be inaccurate or overly biased? (4) Are there any reasons to question the honesty or integrity of the source? The answers to these questions, noted Haskins, should inform an individual as to whether to accept the information a source provides, another skill central to critical thinking.

Step 5: Evaluation of Arguments

To complete his skill-based model of critical thinking, Haskins asserted that the evaluation of arguments is a three-step process that assesses whether (1) assumptions are warranted, (2) reasoning is relevant and sufficient, and (3) relevant information has been omitted. With respect to (1), Haskins characterized a "warranted" assumption as one that is either known to be true or is sufficiently reasonable to accept without the requirement of additional information to support it. He noted that, should a critical thinker be unable to locate research to support the presumption of truth of information, rather than reject an assumption, he or she should evaluate whether the claim is reasonable in terms of his or her own experience, as well as the source and nature of the assumption itself. The direct relevance to evidence-based clinical practice is clear. With respect to (2), Haskins noted the need to assess relevance (i.e., quality) and sufficiency (i.e., quantity) of reasoning. Whether reasoning is topically and logically related and substantive enough to validate an argument is a crucial determination for the critical thinker, who must reflect upon the purpose for the argument, as well as the contemporary standards for the evaluation of the evidence used to support that argument and whether the strength of the evidence is proportional to the strength of the claim that is asserted, with no relevant evidence suppressed or excluded from consideration.

Model #2: Wyckoff

Wyckoff (2012) conceptualized critical thinking skills as "core competencies" that he wanted to instill in the students in his university-level classes. His skill model for critical thinking included these competencies:

(a) The Ability to Think Empirically, not Theoretically. Wyckoff described this as the ability of students to constantly check their views in relation to evidence from the real world and the courage to change their positions if improved explanations appear.

(b) The Ability to Think in Terms of Multiple, Rather than Single, Causes. Wyckoff noted that, in their single-cause explanations for events, students have not considered the effects of intervening variables on those events and thus render their explanations suspect.

(c) The Ability to Think in Terms of the Sizes of Things, Rather than Only in Terms of Their Direction. Wyckoff posited that in a world of relatively magnitude-free debates, decisions could benefit from the infusion of information about sizes of various effects on events.
(d) The Ability to Think like "Foxes," Not "Hedgehogs." Wyckoff characterized hedgehogs as those who know one "big thing" and apply that understanding to everything around them and compared them with foxes, who know many "small things" and apply this "grab bag" of knowledge to their predictions about the world.
(e) The Ability to Understand One's Own Biases. Wyckoff asserted that humans possess many unconscious biases and that a failure to understand these biases contributes to poor decisions. He pinpointed "confirmation bias," or the tendency to seek out information compatible with previous views and to dismiss information contrary to previous views.

Model #3: Halpern

Halpern (2014) specified a number of skills that reflect critical thinking. Several relate to how a thinker deals with information: ability to read and write complex information, retrieval of relevant information as needed, identification of "semantic slants" applied to words, determination of credibility of sources of information, identification of contradictions in evidence used to support positions, synthesis of information from a variety of sources, provisions of reasons for style and quantity of information provided to individuals across different contexts, mastery of basic research methods in use of quantitative information to express ideas, and use of visual matrices and other models to convey information. Others represented learning, such as how one acquires new skills and relates new information to previously learned ideas, as well as how one monitors his or her own learning to decide when support would be valuable. And, others represented some outcomes of thinking, such as evaluating risk versus benefit, developing reasonable methods for selecting from among alternative courses of action, and presenting persuasive arguments on topics.

Model #4: Critical Thinking Initiative

The Critical Thinking Initiative (CTI) of the Nashville State Community College (NSCC) (n.d.) noted, ". . . When we think, we seek the truth" (n.p.). Toward this end, the CTI adopted the definition of critical thinking as "careful and deliberate determination of whether to accept, reject, or suspend judgment." To enable students to strive closer to this end, the CTI specified four fundamental skills required of every critical thinker: analysis, evaluation, inference, and deduction.

Analysis, according to CTI, is scrutinizing parts of a whole for their relevance and significance. CTI noted that analysis allows a thinker to separate the evidence an individual has provided from his or her conclusions, then to determine whether the totality of the evidence is compatible with these conclusions. The focus of analysis can be words, data, facts, or other entities. No matter what the focus, the intention of a critical thinker is to understand not only that an individual holds a belief but to understand why he or she embraces that concept.

Evaluation, according to CTI, is making judgments according to appropriate criteria. CTI noted that evaluation allows a thinker to determine how strong or weak an argument is or how believable a given statement is. The CTI further noted that a critical thinker should be able to answer such questions as how he or she would decide an issue, how he or she would prove or argue a position, whether the available information was sufficient as the basis for an informed judgment, what conclusion he or she would draw from this available information, what critique he or she would offer for this available information, and how he or she would justify a position.

Inference, according to CTI, involves hypothesizing and developing conclusions based upon facts, reasons, observations, and evidence. CTI noted that inference allows the application of both deductive and inductive skills to evaluation of beliefs, opinions, facts, conjectures, principles, and assumptions. The CTI further noted that a critical thinker should be able to answer such questions as why a person behaved in a particular way, what the consequence is of the available information, and how the available information supports a conclusion.

Deduction, according to CTI, involves using generalizations to draw conclusions applicable to a specific situation. The CTI noted that, while a thinker may not be able to be 100% certain about any conclusion, he or she may be reasonably certain about the validity of conclusions reached from deduction. The CTI further noted that a critical thinker should be able to answer such questions as what the premises or generalizations are in the present situation, what the conclusion is that someone has reached based upon these premises, whether the premises are true, and whether the premises provide sufficient support for the conclusion.

Model #5: The American Philosophical Association

The American Philosophical Association (APA) produced a document named the "APA Delphi Report" (Facione, 1990), which summarized the results of a two-year project to articulate an international expert consensus definition of critical thinking and delineate its "core cognitive skills." These skills were interpretation, analysis, evaluation, inference, explanation, and self-regulation. A brief definition, based upon the Delphi Report, follows for each skill.

Interpretation is "to comprehend and express the meaning or significance of a wide variety of experiences, situations, data, events, judgments, conventions, beliefs, rules, procedures, or criteria" (p. 6).

Analysis is "to identify the intended and actual inferential relationships among statements, questions, concepts, descriptions, or other forms of representation intended to express belief, judgment, experiences, reasons, information, or opinions" (p. 7).

Evaluation is "to assess the credibility of statements or other representations which are accounts or descriptions of a person's perception, experience, situation, judgment, belief, or opinion; and to assess the logical strength of the actual or intended inferential relationships among statements, descriptions, questions, or other forms of representation" (p. 8).

Inference is "to identify and secure elements needed to draw reasonable conclusions; to form conjectures and hypotheses; to consider relevant information and to deduce the consequences flowing from data, statements, principles, evidence, judgments, beliefs, opinions, concepts, descriptions, questions, or other forms of representations" (p. 9).

Explanation is "to present in a cogent and coherent way the results of one's reasoning" (p. 10).

Self-Regulation is to "self-consciously monitor one's cognitive activities, the elements used in those activities, and the results educed, particularly by applying skills in analysis, and evaluation to one's own inferential judgments with a view toward questioning, confirming, validating, or correcting either one's responding or one's results." Self-Regulation, in effect, "allows good critical thinkers to improve their own thinking. In a sense this is critical thinking applied to itself" (p. 11).

Model #6: Halonen

Halonen (1996) conceptualized three domains within critical thinking and described the basic skills that students must possess for success in each of these domains: practical, theoretical, and methodological.

Practical domain: Students apply critical thinking skills to practical situations to become "wise consumers, more careful judges of character, or more cautious interpreters of behavior." They distinguish what they observe (i.e., the question of what is the behavior observed) from the inferences they draw from what they observe (i.e., the question of what is the meaning of the behavior observed). As a result, they become less confident in their immediate conclusions, more tolerant of ambiguity in situations, and more likely to propose alternative explanations.

Theoretical domain: Students develop appreciation for scientific explanations of behavior. They acquire not only the content of their discipline but also the concepts, principles, laws, and theories. They then move into application of these theories to actual situations as they attempt to interpret the situation (such as a clinical case) via the lenses of multiple perspectives. They then move into evaluation of theories as they select or reject theories based on their systematic evaluation based on evidence and reason. More advanced studies help them create their own theory-based explanations for behavior as they synthesize and integrate current theories and incorporate new insights into these.

Methodological domain: Students apply varied research methods. They start with acquisition of information about the scientific method. This enables their identification of specific design elements in existing research. From there, they move into evaluation of the quality of specific designs and the validity of specific research conclusions. Eventually, they will develop and execute their own research designs, initially with close mentorship and ultimately independently.

Careful review of these examples of "skills models" will reveal some common elements. The models include specific critical thinking skills, which the authors have often compiled into categories or domains as a way to identify the themes that integrate the skills into the critical thinking process. While useful to explain the skills that can be the focus of evaluation of the sophistication of critical thinking, even now no definitive skills model has been embraced.

Disposition Model

Yet another approach to conceptualization of critical thinking focuses upon the identification of dispositions that are relevant to the critical thinking process. These models presume that, if individuals demonstrate particular tendencies—either those that appear to be "natural" to them or those that they have learned from experience and practice—they will then be successful in various critical thinking tasks. We now overview representative "disposition models" whose creators have attempted to describe the dispositions that are essential to successful critical thinking.

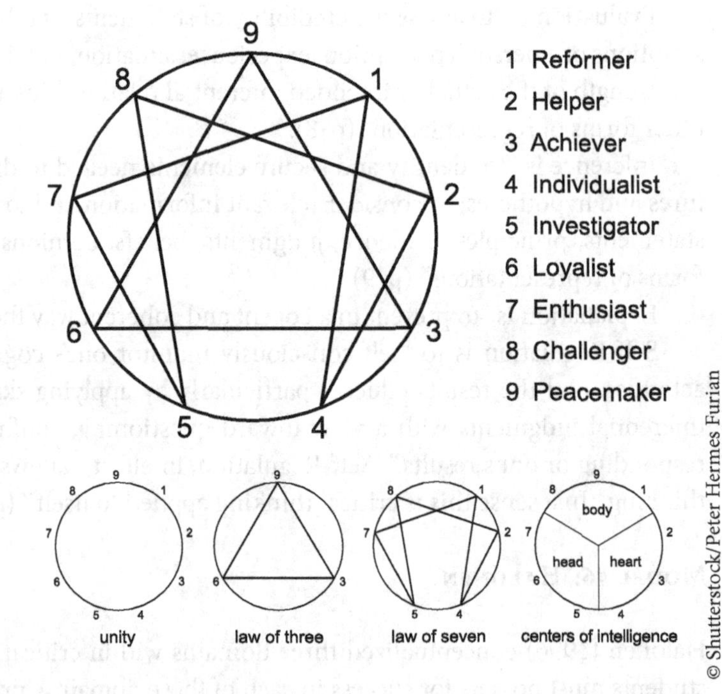

Model #1: Glaser

In his seminal work on the role of critical thinking in education, Glaser (1941) noted that the ability to think critically involves, "(1) an attitude of being disposed to consider in a thoughtful way the problems and subjects that come within the range of one's experiences, (2) knowledge of the methods of logical inquiry and reasoning, and (3) some skill in applying those methods" (p. 6). While Glaser did not develop his concept of dispositions into a detailed model, his observations stimulated further discussions of whether individuals possess natural inclinations that increase the likelihood that they will apply critical thinking to the situations they face in day-to-day interactions.

Model #2: National Council for Excellence in Critical Thinking

The National Council for Excellence in Critical Thinking (NCECT) (1987) noted two components of critical thinking, (1) a set of information and belief-generating and processing skills (in contrast to the simple acquisition and retention of information alone) and (2) the intellectual commitment to using those skills to guide behavior (in contrast to the simple possession and use of skills without acceptance of their results). As was the case with Glaser, the NCECT did not create a detailed model. However, their deliberations acknowledged that skills without dispositions would not, by definition, be sufficient for successful critical thinking, as dispositions provided the motivation for application.

Model #3: Giancarlo and Facione

Giancarlo and Facione (2001) questioned the description of critical thinking as an outcome of cognitive skills with their assertion that, "Any conceptualization of critical thinking that focuses exclusively on cognitive skills is incomplete. A more comprehensive view of critical thinking must include the acknowledgement of a characterological component, often referred to as a disposition, to describe a person's inclination to use critical thinking when faced with problems to solve, ideas to evaluate, or decisions to make . . . The disposition toward critical thinking, as a dimension of personality, refers to the likelihood that one will approach problem framing or problem solving by using reasoning. Thus, the disposition toward critical thinking is the consistent internal motivation to engage problems and make decisions by using thinking" (p. 31).

Model #4: American Philosophical Association Delphi Report

In the description of the previous kind of model, a skills-based model, we summarized a list of skills identified in the APA Delphi Report (Facione, 1990). As we noted, this report was the result of a two-year collaborative discussion of experts from across academic disciplines who attempted to define critical thinking for the benefit of those who would be instructing university-level classes. These experts did not restrict their concept of critical thinking to the skills involved, however; they included a discussion of the disposition of those most likely to employ critical thinking.

They used the term "critical spirit" to mean "a probing inquisitiveness, a keenness of mind, a zealous dedication to reason, and a hunger or eagerness for reliable information" (p. 11). They further compiled a list of "approaches to life and living" that characterize critical thinking: inquisitiveness with regard to a wide range of issues; concern to become and remain well informed; alertness to opportunities to use critical thinking; trust in the processes of reasoned inquiry; self-confidence in one's own abilities to reason; open-mindedness regarding divergent worldviews; flexibility in considering alternatives and opinions; understanding of the opinions of other people; fair-mindedness in appraising reasoning; honesty in facing one's own biases, prejudices, stereotypes, or egocentric tendencies; prudence in suspending, making, or altering judgments;

and willingness to reconsider and revise views where honest reflection suggests that change is warranted. They added to this list another list of ways that "good" critical thinkers approach specific issues, questions, or problems: clarity in stating the question or concern, orderliness in working with complexity, diligence in seeking relevant information, reasonableness in selecting and applying criteria, care in focusing attention on the concern at hand, persistence though difficulties are encountered, and precision to the degree permitted by the subject and the circumstances.

In their discussion of dispositions, the experts differentiated between individuals with a "strong" disposition toward critical thinking and those without a "strong" disposition in terms of their reactions to sample statements. For instance, someone with a "strong" disposition, according to the experts, would agree with statements like, "Making intelligent decisions is more important than winning arguments" and "I try to see the merit in another's opinion, even if I reject it later." In contrast, someone without a "strong" disposition, according to the experts, would agree with statements like, "I prefer jobs where the supervisor says exactly what to do and exactly how to do it" and "I hate when teachers discuss problems instead of just giving the answers." While the experts who generated the results in the APA Delphi Report reached consensus in their answers to many questions related to critical thinking, they were unable to completely see eye-to-eye on the interpretation of the word "good." This word carried many connotations, some of which were connected with moral and ethical standards. Ultimately, the majority of the experts expressed the view that effective critical thinking did not possess a 1:1 correlation with cultural beliefs, religious tenets, ethical values, social mores, political orientations, or orthodoxies of any kind. Instead, the commitment to seek the truth in an objective, fair-minded fashion was the undercurrent of critical thinking. The experts did, however, acknowledge that any person can, unfortunately, use any skill either ethically or unethically, with the hope being that critical thinking becomes a tool for the improvement rather than the detriment of society. The APA Delphi Report extended the previous research in that, rather than a model alone, the experts presented implications for instruction in critical thinking, accompanied by concrete recommendations for educational experiences that enhance dispositions.

MODEL #5: ENNIS

Ennis (1991) developed a model based upon his definition of critical thinking as "reasonable reflective thinking that is focused on deciding what to believe or do" (p. 6). His model started with "Problem Solving Context," or the circumstances that surround the presentation of the problem to be addressed. His model continued with the reference to "Critical Thinking Dispositions." Within his model, as did some other scholars, he differentiated critical thinking dispositions from critical thinking abilities. These dispositions are the basis for two aspects of problem solving. One is clarity, or the ability one has to clearly state the problem to be addressed, while the other is the supposition of alternatives rather than simply one potential solution. His model continued into the "Basis for Decision," and he noted that the integration of information from others (indirect), information from observation (direct), and reference to previously drawn acceptable conclusions forms the core of evidence to support an ultimate decision. In the next component of his model, "Inference," the thinker applies both deduction and induction to the examination of evidence and imposes value judgments upon these data. The ultimate outcome of this process is a decision about a belief or an action.

MODEL #6: HALPERN

While Halpern (2014) identified a number of core critical thinking skills (which we described in the previous section), she noted, "No one can become a better thinker just by reading a book or even by just learning a set of thinking skills that would be useful if they were used" (p. 20). She considered the development of the disposition of a critical thinker as an essential component of the critical thinking process and, in fact, considered "attitude" to be a major difference between those at different points on the critical thinking continuum. She identified a number of dispositional traits of critical thinkers:

Critical Thinkers Plan: Rather than react impulsively when placed into situations, critical thinkers plan their responses. With their plans, critical thinkers prevent habitual responses that may not be appropriate for situations, as well as provide "prescriptive descriptions" of what to do to best deal with a situation. While these descriptions may resemble scripts, critical thinkers in fact have multiple options embedded within the broad scripted frameworks.

Critical Thinkers Self-Regulate: Critical thinkers strive toward a goal using feedback, monitoring comprehension, assessing progress, and making judgments about the quantity and quality of their learning.

Critical Thinkers Demonstrate Flexibility: Rather than resist new information, critical thinkers consider new options for situations, as well as reconsider the merits of old options. Flexibility also includes the ability to take the perspective of another individual, consider multiple options, formulate multiple responses, and seek new information that may not be readily available. This necessitates the development of a comfort level with the unknown.

Critical Thinkers Persist: Critical thinkers continue to work toward an end result rather than discontinue their efforts. They allow themselves multiple attempts and learn from each successive trial in a situation.

Critical Thinkers Admit Errors and Self-Correct: Errors are part of the risk involved in consideration of information that leads to solutions for problems. Critical thinkers admit their errors and, in fact, learn from them. Rather than offer self-justification, critical thinkers instead conduct self-criticism in their exploration of where their breakdown in thinking occurred and how this breakdown can be corrected.

Critical Thinkers Are Mindful: Critical thinkers reflect on the processes and products of their own thinking. Rather than application of automatic thinking to situations that demand non-automatic thinking, they discern which situations demand a level of critical reflection and mindfully engage with those situations. They self-monitor both during a situation and after the situation has concluded.

Critical Thinkers Seek Consensus: In their interactions with collections of individuals (such as in committees), critical thinkers consider the obstacles to consensus, then systematically address these obstacles with communication and compromise. Not to be confused with compliance or conformity with popular opinion, critical thinkers reach their conclusions based not on what is popular but instead on what is valid.

Critical Thinkers Transfer Skills: After they develop an extensive repertoire of skills, critical thinkers invest the effort to apply them to situations. Successful application of skills involves the discernment of which skills are most appropriate for which situation. Certainly multiple skills apply to multiple contexts. However, critical thinkers discern the cues within situations that indicate which specific skills would be most appropriate.

In addition to the philosophical discussions of the dispositions of critical thinkers, some scholars have collected empirical evidence to inform the dispositional models. For instance, Krupat, Sprague, Wolpaw, Haidet, Hatern, and O'Brien (2011) explored the question about whether clinical educators agreed on definitions of critical thinking, then whether their descriptions of critical thinking in clinical practice were consistent with their definitions. The study indirectly addressed the question of whether critical thinking reflected skill, disposition, or both, at least as viewed by the clinical educators. Clinical educators (N=97) across five medical schools provided definitions, described clinical scenarios in which critical thinking would be important, and stated actions of practitioners who were and were not thinking critically. The researchers then qualitatively analyzed the content of their responses to identify patterns and themes. A majority of the clinical educators described critical thinking in terms of students' skills rather than dispositions. However, their descriptions of clinical scenarios in which practitioners were not thinking critically reflected breakdowns in dispositions rather than in specific critical thinking skills. Based on these patterns, the authors identified the need for reconciliation of the definitions of critical thinking with the application of critical thinking to clinical scenarios by clinical educators.

In additional research, Scheffer and Rubenfeld (2000) and Rubenfeld and Scheffer (2006) collected qualitative data which then served as the basis for a statement of the critical thinking skills necessary for clinical practice in a specific discipline, nursing. They identified several themes that appeared in the reflections of practitioners: confidence with respect to thinking and reasoning skills, consideration of multiple contextual factors that affect practice, compilation of a collection of creative solutions to issues, implementation of a flexible and adaptable course of action that is open to modification, use of observations and questions to discover and comprehend new information, sincerity in attempts to seek the truth even when it is contrary to prior assumptions and beliefs, reliance on intuition based on interpretations of prior experiences, open-mindedness to alternative views and sensitivity to personal assumptions that can affect reactions, perseverance and determination to overcome obstacles, and contemplation of the process of critical thinking and problem solving to enhance self-evaluation and learning. These themes were consistent with those included in the various models.

As was the case with the "skills models," careful review of these examples of "disposition models" will reveal some common elements. The models include tendencies that critical thinkers have that manifest themselves in specific approaches to gathering information and solving problems. While useful to describe the dispositions that stem from, lead to, and/or interact with critical thinking, as was the case with the "skills models," no definitive disposition model has been embraced.

Stage Model

Another approach to conceptualization of critical thinking focuses upon the description of stages of development of critical thinking. The "stage models" presume that an individual can—either by maturation, experience, or the interaction of both—move to increased levels of sophistication of critical thinking and that these levels are both quantitatively and qualitatively different. We now overview representative "stage models" whose creators have attempted to describe the transitions from one level to the next as success in critical thinking improves.

© Shutterstock/Leremy

Model #1: Bloom

Bloom (1956) created the taxonomy that bears his name and continues to influence educational practices to this day. This taxonomy consists of six levels of learning, which increase in difficulty from a rating of 1 to 6. Although Bloom did not focus on the term "critical thinking," his concepts nonetheless captured the spirit of the descriptions of the nature of critical thinking. A brief overview of each of his levels of learning follows.

Level 1: Knowledge
Students at this level recall terms, definitions, facts, and rules. In SLP, then, students at Level 1 would learn such information as the names of anatomical structures related to speech production, the definitions of the various elements of oral communication, the names and locations of various professional associations, and the code of conduct for participation in a class.

Level 2: Comprehension
Students at this level move beyond simple retention to manipulation of information. They sort, describe, compare, and explain information. In SLP, then, students at Level 2 would demonstrate their comprehension of information in such tasks as comparing and contrasting the elements of language (such as phonology vs. morphology) or explaining the phases of the swallowing process.

Level 3: Application
Students at this level apply previously acquired information to new scenarios for which the previous information could be relevant. In SLP, then, students at Level 3 would apply information in such endeavors as the oral-facial examination, acoustic analyses of voice production, linguistic analysis of parent–child interaction, evaluation of two patients with similar histories, treatment of two patients with identical diagnoses, or interpretation of the literature.

Level 4: Analysis
Students at this level study evidence with the potential to support presumptions in an attempt to reach a reasonable conclusion. In SLP, then, students at Level 4 would analyze a variety of kinds of evidence: case history information, speech sample transcripts, hearing screening reports, bedside swallow studies, norm-referenced test results, previous clinical reports, expert testimony, and quantitative and qualitative studies published in the literature.

Level 5: Synthesis
Students at this level use previous information to develop solutions, products, or proposals. In SLP, then, students at Level 5 would synthesize information from a number of sources to prepare reviews of the literature, proposals for research studies, evaluation or treatment plans, resource-efficient clinical schedules, innovative service delivery models, new evaluation or treatment protocols, or community education initiatives.

Level 6: Evaluation
Students at this level make quantitative and qualitative judgments as they demonstrate critical thinking. In SLP, then, students at Level 6 would evaluate their own academic performance as they review their papers or their examinations, as well as conduct perceptive evaluations for the clinical performance of both themselves and their peers. They would identify relative areas of competence, as well as steps to remedy deficiencies.

Model #2: Meyers

Meyers (1986) asserted that critical thinking is discipline related. That is, students learn critical thinking relevant to their academic disciplines as they learn the terms, concepts, issues, and methods applicable to their disciplines. With that said, however, he also placed critical thinking into the broader context of cognitive development, specifically as related to a Piagetian framework. Before we overview the conclusions of Meyers, an overview of the stages of Piaget is in order.

Piaget conceptualized stages of cognitive development and associated these with broad age ranges in individuals.

Stage 1 – Sensorimotor: Piaget equated this stage of development with infants. Within this period, infants demonstrate their cognitive skills in their motor movements. As this period unfolds, infants develop a number of skills that are precursors for more advanced, symbolic skills. These include joint attention, object permanence, and means-end behavior. Such precursors appear to enhance language development, as they relate directly to specific language skills (such as the use of symbolic words for naming items, individuals, and ideas).

Stage 2 – Pre-Operations: Piaget equated this stage of development with toddlers and preschool children. Within this period, children demonstrate their cognitive skills in their symbolic behaviors particularly their language and their imagination. Piaget characterized their thinking at this point as both non-logical and non-reversible thought. Specific characteristics of their thinking include (a) dependence on perception for interpretation of situation, (b) focus on an individual aspect of a situation, (c) focus on states of items rather than on their transformations, and (d) and inability to reverse conditions back to an original state. Their thinking appears random rather than systematic.

Stage 3 – Concrete Operations: Piaget equated this stage of development with elementary and secondary school children. Within this period, children demonstrate their cognitive skills in their interactions with concrete (or physical) items. Children perform sequences of logical behavior but apply these only to what is seen, not to what is represented mentally. In contrast to their egocentric perspective of the pre-operational stage, in which they viewed the world in reference to their own perspective, children start to decenter and at least attempt to view situations from the perspectives of others. Additionally, children start to demonstrate conservation, or appreciation that an item remains the same even if its appearance is altered in some way. They also manipulate symbols, such as words, related to concrete items, and they develop the ability to reverse conditions of items back to an original state.

Stage 4 – Formal Operations: Piaget equated this stage of development with secondary school children onward into adulthood. Within this period, children and adults demonstrate their cognitive skills in higher-order reasoning. Such reasoning involves independence from concrete items, as children and adults can now perform cognitive operations in their minds without reference to the physical world. This level is characterized by such skills as (a) categorization of items, individuals, and ideas according to a variety of properties, (b) systematic manipulation of variables to test hypotheses about a situation, (c) appreciations of connections between behaviors and their outcomes, and (d) application of logical thought and deductive reasoning. A formal thinker links previous experiences, present circumstances, and anticipated consequences to maximize the opportunities for successful navigation of situations.

Meyers equated critical thinking with reaching the level of "formal operations" conceived by Piaget (1972). He noted that students move through various cycles in their educational experiences, starting with concrete explorations of materials, followed by raising questions and generating hypotheses to be applied to generate abstract concepts and principles. Meyers also noted that, in addition to cognitive development, ethical development (as in the form of personal values) and personal style (as in curiosity and a desire to order the personal environment) also influence the level of critical thinking one attains and applies. The literature has reported that, unfortunately, many adults never reach the level of formal operations. As early as the 1970s, scholars (e.g., Chiappetta, 1975) questioned the presumption that individuals, as a function of maturation, automatically proceed to formal operations. Chiappetta reviewed a body of literature that supported the idea that over 50% of the American population at 16+ years old still functioned at the level of concrete operations. These data have been confirmed by other scholars. Renner, Stafford, Lawson, McKinnon, Friot, and Kellogg (1976) estimated the percent of students in each of Piaget's levels of cognitive development and characterized approximately 25% of students at the level of formal operations (with approximately 20% at formal-onset and 5% at formal-mature). Similarly, Kuhn, Langer, Kohlberg, and Haan (1997) estimated that only 30–35% of students reach formal operations by the time they finish secondary school. The implications of these data certainly call into question whether the expectation for critical thinking in university-level students is reasonable and, if so, which methods of instruction increase the likelihood of successful application of critical thinking strategies.

Model #3: Halpern, Stephenson, and Williams

Halpern, Stephenson, and Williams (2009), whose definition of critical thinking we included earlier in this section, expanded their work in this area with their creation of a model of critical thinking, which they differentiated from such versions of thinking as random methods, memorization, day dreaming, night dreaming, and "sloppy" thinking.

The authors noted that different kinds of information necessitate different kinds of cognitive processes to appropriately deal with such information. To explain this idea more completely, they created a model of intellectual development with critical thinking at its core. The inspiration for their model was that of Perry (1968), whose model was based upon the results of his survey research of students at Harvard University and Radcliffe College in the 1950s. While his model did not describe critical thinking per se, he did note many characteristics typical of a critical thinker. Based upon this, the current authors divided his model into four developmental stages through which individuals purportedly pass in a linear fashion.

Stage I: Basic Duality

This level of thinking is characterized by the belief that there is one solution to a problem and that the authority of the source of the solution is not to be questioned. Students who demonstrate this level of thinking will strictly memorize material with little to no critical thinking about the material.

Stage II: Multiplicity (Pre-Legitimate)

This level of thinking is characterized by a move away from the belief that there is one solution to the belief that the solution remains to be known and that multiple solutions, in fact, may exist. Students who demonstrate this level of thinking will appreciate that they need to collect evidence to support opinions, which include their own.

Stage III: Relativism (Correlate, Competing, or Diffuse)

This level of thinking is characterized by the appreciation that solutions are contextual, as well as the acceptance of the idea that all knowledge may be relative but not equally valid. Students who demonstrate this level of thinking will realize that theories resemble metaphors for the world and may not constitute absolute truths.

Stage IV: Commitment Foreseen

This level of thinking is characterized by the commitment of students to carefully consider how knowledge is obtained, used, and created. Students who demonstrate this level of thinking both assess and accept new information, become more flexible in their respect for the views of others, and learn new information as they simultaneously examine their own values. The process of students reflecting on their own thinking is often known as metacognition.

Model #4: Kuhn

Kuhn (1999) promoted a developmental model of critical thinking. The heart of her model is metacognition—the assertion that metacognitive, even more than cognitive, skills are essential for effective critical thinking. Kuhn divided the process of "metaknowing" (i.e., when one knows that he or she knows) into three broad categories: metastrategic, metacognitive, and epistemological. She differentiated between procedural knowledge (i.e., knowing how), which corresponds with metastrategic skills, and declarative knowledge (i.e., knowing what), which corresponds with metacognitive skills. She then characterized epistemological knowledge as both general (i.e., the question of whether anyone can know that he or she knows) and specific (i.e., the question of how well a specific person knows what he or she knows). In her elaboration of the nature of metaknowing, Kuhn presented four levels of "epistemological understanding."

Level 1: The Realist
At the "realist" level, a thinker sees assertions as "copies" that represent an external reality. Reality, in his or her view, is directly knowable, and knowledge that is certain comes from an external source. Critical thinking is unnecessary.

Level 2: The Absolutist
At the "absolutist" level, a thinker sees assertions as "facts" that are either correct or incorrect. Reality, in his or her view, remains directly knowable, and knowledge that is certain continues to come from an external source. Critical thinking, while not absolutely necessary, is a tool to assist in the determination of whether facts are accurate.

Level 3: The Multiplist
At the "multiplist" level, a thinker sees assertions as "opinions" for which their holders are accountable. Reality, in his or her view, is the product of minds and may thus not be certain. Critical thinking is not relevant as a tool to assist in the determination of whether opinions are accurate because of their nature as mental products.

Level 4: The Evaluative
At the "evaluative" level, a thinker sees assertions as "judgments" that can be analyzed based upon specific criteria. Reality, in his or her view, remains the product of minds and thus continues to not be certain. Critical thinking becomes a tool in the comprehension of assertions and the evaluation of their soundness.

Model #5: Paul and Elder

Paul and Elder (1997) and Elder and Paul (2010) argued that predictable stages of critical thinking exist: unreflective, challenged, beginning, practicing, advanced, and master. They asserted that (a) every person who develops as a critical thinker passes through these stages, (b) to pass from one stage to the next depends upon a commitment of an individual to develop as a thinker, (c) to pass from one stage to the next will probably not take place in a subconscious fashion but will, instead, take place via conscious effort, (d) success in instruction is correlated to the quality of critical thinking a student learns, and (e) a student may regress as well as progress in his or her critical thinking. Description of their six proposed stages follows:

Stage 1 – The Unreflective Thinkers: The "unreflective" thinkers are unaware of the role of thinking in their existence, as well as the ways that problems with thinking cause them problems across situations.

Those who are unreflective may have, in fact, developed some critical thinking skills. However, they have not identified these skills as such and therefore do not label their own concepts, assumptions, and inferences. Because of that, they have not developed standards for the evaluation of their own thinking, nor methods for the improvement of their own approaches to reasoning. They also have not developed consistent self-monitoring as a means of discerning whether their approaches are working effectively. And, even if they have developed critical skills, they have not applied these consistently within and across situations, which has resulted in the perception of their skills as random.

Stage 2 – The Challenged Thinkers: The "challenged" thinkers have started to become aware of the role of thinking in their existence and the problems with thinking that cause them problems. Those who are challenged have also started to become aware of their own thinking in terms of the skills presently in their repertoires and the flaws with these skills. However, while they realize their thinking is flawed, they may not know how their thinking is flawed. They have started to appreciate that critical thinking is not an automatic process but rather the result of deliberate thinking about their own thinking. They may also have realized the difference between what they understand and what they do not understand. However, they remain unable to conceptualize standards for how to systematically evaluate their own thinking, which may result in their over- or underestimation of their own level of critical skill.

Stage 3 – The Beginning Thinkers: The "beginning" thinkers have taken some initial responsibility for the quality of their thinking. They have accepted the fact of their limitations and have started to understand how they can overcome barriers to the application of critical thinking. Toward this end, they have started to alter their reactions to situations that necessitate reasoning and problem solving. However, because of their inexperience, they remain inconsistent in their reactions because they do not systematically test the consequences of various courses of action. And, while capable to some extent, they remain inconsistent in how regularly they self-monitor and self-evaluate their thinking. To their credit, they have started to identify their own points of view that influence their thinking and the need to consider other points of view. They continue to need to develop critical thinking as a habitual practice.

Stage 4 – The Practicing Thinkers: The "practicing" thinkers have come to understand that they are responsible for their own thinking. Specifically, they know that both problems and solutions exist and that part of their task is identification of the problems and application of the solutions. They have also committed themselves to more systematic and conscious practice of critical thinking across situations, as well as monitoring and correcting their thinking. However, because of their limited experience with this level of thinking, they are challenged by more abstract or complex problem solving demands and may not monitor or correct their thinking in these situations as accurately as for that in simple tasks. Because of that, continued modeling from and mentoring by more capable thinkers would provide the context-related scaffolding that could advance their critical thinking skills further.

Stage 5 – The Advanced Thinkers: The "advanced" thinkers have made critical thinking a daily way of life. They have been motivated by the benefits they have experienced from this approach to problems and situations. They can articulate their accomplishments with respect to thinking, as well as their continued limitations in the process. While they may apply systematic principles to the majority of situations they encounter, they continue to experience some difficulties with information that is particularly abstract, scenarios that are particularly complicated, or issues that are decidedly unfamiliar. However, at this level they have become more aware of the nature of their difficulties, as well as more able to identify why such difficulties have arisen. Because of that, they have become more competent with the creation of systematic plans for the improvement of their thinking that are consistent with their personal values.

Stage 6 – The Accomplished Thinkers: The "accomplished" thinkers are distinguished by their competency and consistency. For them, monitoring and revising their thinking are routine strategies that lead to continuous improvement in their skills. At both the conscious and subconscious levels, they approach situations in a systematic fashion. They strive toward deeper levels of comprehension of information, which allows them to develop innovative insights into both problems and solutions. Their thinking is characterized by clarity, accuracy, precision, and relevance and is based upon principles, not on situational expediency. While not perfect (for no human can attain perfection), their thinking can serve as a model for others with respect to seeking, evaluating, interpreting, and applying information across a diverse assortment of conditions.

MODEL #6: GARRISON

Garrison (1992), who approached critical thinking as problem solving, presented a five-stage model of critical thinking skills: (1) problem identification, (2) problem definition, (3) problem exploration, (4) problem evaluation, and (5) problem integration. Garrison labeled Stage 1, Problem Identification, as "elementary clarification." At this level, individuals observe a problem that has arisen, then describe its central elements. He then labeled Stage 2, Problem Definition, as "in-depth clarification." At this level, individuals frame the problem and propose solutions, with these solutions based primarily on the prior experiences of both the individuals and those whom they consult. They also identify values and assumptions that appear to underlie the problem at hand. Garrison labeled Stage 3, Problem Exploration, as "inference." Individuals apply both induction and deduction to the situation at hand, as well as creatively provide as many resolutions as possible to the problem. He then labeled Stage 4, Problem Evaluation, as "judgment." Individuals now evaluate pros and cons of each possible resolution, as well as anticipate the consequences should particular solutions be applied to problems. For the final aspect of his model, Stage 5, Problem Integration, which he labeled "strategy formation," Garrison noted that individuals coordinate the application of solutions to a problem, then participate in follow-up evaluation as needed. We noted that, while the word "problem" often carries less than positive connotations, Garrison simply used this word to indicate a situation that necessitated a solution, which could, in fact, be the catalyst for positive actions and accomplishments.

As was the case with both the "skills models" and the "disposition models," careful review of these examples of "stage models" will reveal some common elements: the presumption that critical thinking skills can be learned, the observation that skills evolve both quantitatively and qualitatively, the notation that not every individual reaches every level of critical thinking expertise, and that advancement in competence mandates conscious efforts. These models are as useful as the previous kinds of models to explain critical thinking. However, as was the case with the previous models, no definitive stage model has been embraced. Clearly, the need for continued examination of the progression of critical thinking skills exists.

REFERENCES

Bailin, S., Case, R., Coombs, J. R., & Daniels, L. B. (1999). Conceptualizing critical thinking. Journal of Curriculum Studies, 31(3), 285-302.

Bergmann, M., Moor, J., & Nelson, J. (2009). The logic book (5th ed.). New York, NY: McGraw-Hill Publishers.

Bloom, B. S. (Ed.). (1956). Taxonomy of educational objects (vols. 1 and 2). New York, NY: David McKay Publishers.

Chiappetta, E. L. (1975). A perspective on formal thought development. Paper presented to the Annual Meeting of the National Association for Research in Science Teaching, Los Angeles, CA.

Education Portal, The. (n.d.). What is critical thinking? Definition-skills-meaning. Available from http://education-portal.com/academy/lesson/what-is-critical-thinking-definition-skills-meaning.html. Retrieved 10/15/2014.
Elder, L. (2007). Defining critical thinking. Available from http://www.criticalthinking.org/pages/defining-critical-thinking/766. Retrieved 10/15/2014.
Elder, L., & Paul, R. (2010). A stage theory of critical thinking. Available from http://www.criticalthinking.org/pages/critical-thinking-development-a-stage-theory/483. Retrieved 10/15/2014.
Ennis, R. H. (1991). Critical thinking: A streamlined conception. Teaching Philosophy, 14, 5-25.
Facione, P. A. (1990). Critical thinking: A statement of expert consensus for purposes of educational assessment and instruction. Millbrae, CA: The California Academic Press.
Facione, P. A. (2006). Critical thinking: What it is and why it counts. San Jose, CA: Insight Assessment.
Garrison, D. R. (1991). Critical thinking and adult education: A conceptual model for developing critical thinking in adult learners. International Journal of Lifelong Education, 10(4), 287-305.
Garrison, D. R. (1992). Critical thinking and self-directed learning in adult education: An analysis of responsibility and control issues. Adult Education Quarterly, 42(3), 136-148.
Geng, F. (2014). A content analysis of the definition of critical thinking. Asian Social Science, 10(19), 124-128.
Giancarlo, C. A., & Facione, P. A. (2001). A look at four years at the disposition toward critical thinking among undergraduate students. The Journal of General Education, 50 (1), 29-55.
Glaser, E. (1941). An experiment in the development of critical thinking. New York, NY: Columbia University Press.
Halonen, J. S. (1996). On critical thinking. Observer, 9(4), 6-8.
Halpern, D. F. (2014). Thought and knowledge: An introduction to critical thinking (5th ed.). New York, NY: Taylor and Francis Press.
Halpern, D., Stephenson, C., & Williams, P. (2009). Critical thinking. Available from http://www.education.com/reference/article/critical-thinking/. Retrieved 10/15/2014.
Haskins, G. R. (2013). A practical guide to critical thinking. Available from http://www.scribd.com/doc/52700999/Haskins-Greg-A-Practical-Guide-to-Critical-Thinking. Retrieved 10-15-2014.
Krupat, E., Sprague, J. M., Wolpaw, D., Haidet, P., Hatern, D., & O'Brien, B. (2011). Thinking critically about critical thinking: Ability, disposition, or both? Medical Education, 45(6), 625-635.
Kuhn, D. (1999). A developmental model of critical thinking. Educational Researcher, 28(2), 16-25.
Kuhn, D., Langer, J., Kohlberg, L., & Haan, N. S. (1977). The development of formal operations in logical and moral judgment. Genetic Psychology Monographs, 95, 97-188.
Lipman, M. (1988). Critical thinking – what can it be? Educational Leadership, 46, 38-43.
Meyers, C. (1986). Teaching students to think critically: A guide for faculty in all disciplines. Hoboken, NJ: Jossey-Bass Higher Education Publishers.
Moon, J. (2005). We seek it here: A new perspective on the elusive activity of critical thinking. Heslington, York, UK: HEA Subject Centre for Education.
Moore, T. (2011). Critical thinking: Seven definitions in search of a concept. Studies in Higher Education, 38(4), 506-522.
Mulnix, J. W. (2012). Thinking critically about critical thinking. Educational Philosophy and Theory, 44(5), 464-479.
Nashville State Community College. (n.d.). Critical thinking initiative. Available from http://ww2.nscc.edu/criticalthinking_forstudents/ta_ctdef.htm. Retrieved 10/15/2014.
National Council for Excellence in Critical Thinking. (1987). Defining critical thinking. Available from http://www.criticalthinking.org/pages/defining-critical-thinking/410. Retrieved 10/15/2014.
Nordquist, R. (n.d.). Critical thinking. Available from http://grammar.about.com/od/c/g/Critical-Thinking.htm. Retrieved 10/15/2014.
Paul, R., & Elder, L. (1997). Critical thinking: Implications for instruction of the stage theory. Journal of Developmental Education, 20(3), 34-35.
Paul, R., & Elder, L. (2001). Critical thinking: Tools for taking charge of your learning and your life. San Jose, CA: Insight Assessment.
Paul, R., & Elder, L. (2008). The miniature guide to critical thinking concepts and tools. Tomales, CA: Foundation for Critical Thinking Press.
Perry, W. (1968). Forms of intellectual and ethical development: In the college years. New York, NY: Holt, Rinehart, and Winston.

Piaget, J. (1972). The psychology of the child. New York, NY: Basic Books.

Renner, J., Stafford, D., Lawson, A., McKinnon, J., Friot, E., & Kellogg, D. (1976). Research, teaching, and learning with the Piaget model. Norman, OK: The University of Oklahoma Press.

Robinson, J. H. (1921). The mind in the making: The relation of intelligence to social reform. New York, NY: Harper & Brothers Publishers.

Rubenfeld, M., & Scheffer, B. (2006). Critical thinking tactics for nurses. Boston, MA: Jones and Bartlett Publishers.

Saiz, C., & Rivas, S. F. (2008). Assessment in critical thinking: A proposal for differentiating ways of thinking. Ergo, 22, 25-66.

Sanders, M., & Moulenbelt, J. (2011). Defining critical thinking. Inquiry, 26(1), 38-46.

Scheffer, B., & Rubenfeld, M. (2000). A consensus statement on critical thinking in nursing. Journal of Nursing Education, 39, 253-359.

Scriven, M., & Paul, R. (1987). Defining critical thinking. Available from http://www.criticalthinking.org/pages/defining-critical-thinking/766. Retrieved 10/15/2014.

Wyckoff, G. (2012). What exactly is critical thinking. Washington, DC: Inside Higher Education. Available from https://www.insidehighered.com/views/2012/10/11/essay-what-political-campaign-shows-about-need-critical-thinking. Retrieved 10/15/2014.

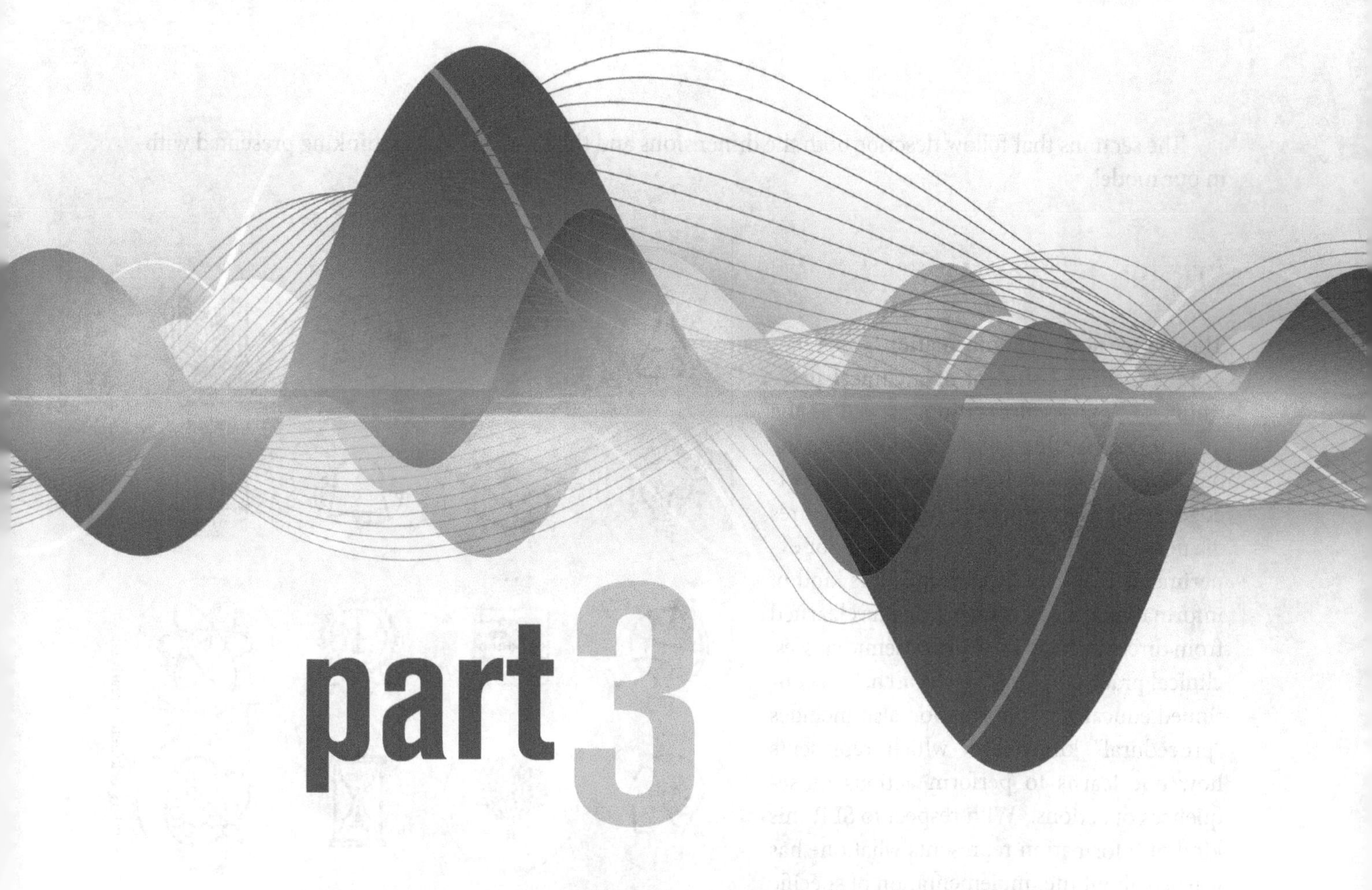

part 3

OVERVIEW OF CRITICAL THINKING MODEL AREAS OF SKILL – LEVELS OF SKILL

As is apparent from our review of definitions and descriptions of critical thinking, varied models of critical thinking exist in the literature. Our aim in the presentation of our model is not to claim that these previous models have substantial deficiencies, for these do not. In fact, these have informed and inspired our model. Our aim is the creation of a tool for clinical practitioners and clinical educators that will allow them to ascertain the level of critical thinking that they or those whom they instruct demonstrate in two dimensions central to clinical practice in SLP, the process of evaluation and the process of intervention, a determination which is the basis for continued development.

Our tool includes broad dimensions of critical thinking: Information, Innovation, Interpretation, Integration, and Intentionality. In response to a prompt (described later), a clinical student or clinical practitioner completes a task and, we trust, includes elements of each of these dimensions of critical thinking in response to the prompt. In the response, the student or practitioner demonstrates a particular level of critical thinking, which for some individuals is uniform across dimensions but for others is uneven from one dimension to the next. Our tool includes four broad levels of sophistication that he or she may demonstrate: Inexperienced, Imitative, Inquisitive, and Ingenious.

The sections that follow describe both the dimensions and the levels of critical thinking presented within our model.

SECTION 1: INFORMATION

© Shutterstock/denk creative

The dimension of "information" references how a clinical student or a clinical practitioner acquires information, as well as the quantity and quality of information he or she has. Information includes "personal" knowledge, which is information that one acquires via personal experiences, observations, or experiments. With respect to SLP, this kind of information represents what one has learned from direct participation in academic classes, clinical practice, scholarly research, and continued education. Information also includes "procedural" knowledge, which represents how one learns to perform actions or sequences of actions. With respect to SLP, this kind of information represents what one has learned about the implementation of specific clinical procedures and the application of specific clinical skills, such as test administration, sample collection, oral examination, and materials presentation. Information also includes "philosophical" knowledge, which is information that one acquires that is factual or theoretical. With respect to SLP, this kind of information represents what one has learned about typical and atypical communication processes, as well as about the theories that attempt to explain the nature of these processes. Appreciation for the literature of the discipline is central to philosophical knowledge. Lastly, information also includes "professional" knowledge, which is information that one acquires related to the standards inherent to a clinical practice discipline. With respect to SLP, this kind of information represents what is contained in cardinal documents of professional associations, as well as the provisions within local, state, and federal laws and the policies enforced by various bodies, such as licensure boards. In addition to these variations of information, this dimension of critical thinking includes the skills that represent information literacy and the ability to access relevant information.

SECTION 2: INNOVATION

The dimension of "innovation" represents how a clinical student or a clinical practitioner creates the most extensive collection of possible courses of action to address a situation. Innovation involves "divergence" in thinking. Divergence is characterized by expansion of thinking that reflects a variety of characteristics. Divergent thinkers are well versed in the current options available to address a situation and means for expansion of these options. With respect to clinical practice in SLP, this translates to, for example, familiarity

© Shutterstock/mrfiza

with current evaluation and treatment methods and materials and articulation of ways that these can be embellished. Divergent thinkers are determined to generate as many ideas as possible to address a situation and have the ability to produce these ideas quickly. With respect to clinical practice in SLP, this represents openness to creation of a variety of ideas to address the same situation, even if those ideas appear in direct opposition to each other. Complementary to this, divergent thinkers create not only simple but also intricate and multifaceted ideas. With respect to clinical practice in SLP, this is represented in not only individual evaluation or treatment components but also interwoven evaluation or treatment plans. Divergent thinkers are open to promote "new" applications of "old" ideas, as well as ideas that are extremely different from what presently exists. With respect to clinical practice in SLP, this flexibility involves new applications for a particular disorder of clinical methods and materials that are traditionally associated with another disorder. Divergent thinkers do not fear the notions that they stand apart, take risks, probe ideas, and question the status quo. Instead, they aim to exhaust every possibility—no matter how superficially unlikely—to arrive at a creative solution.

SECTION 3: INTERPRETATION

The dimension of "interpretation" references how a clinical student or a clinical practitioner systematically analyzes information. Interpretation involves the overview of information that one has accumulated to determine which concepts are accurate vs. inaccurate, complete vs. incomplete, similar vs. dissimilar, objective vs. subjective, consistent vs. inconsistent, and relevant vs. irrelevant to the situation at hand. As critical thinkers interpret information, they also structure the concepts based on whether these are subordinate or superordinate in relation to each other. They also consider the circumstances that surround that information, attentive to the characteristics of the source, the historical context, the theoretical foundation, the extent of internal consistency, the level of academic or professional acceptance, the prior tests of validity and veracity, and the need for and directions of further explorations of the topic. They also reflect on their own expertise and experience and how those have influenced their own perceptions and, by extension, biases in their approach to analysis of information. They specifically identify their emotional and non-emotional biases, such as their personal approach(es) to analysis of information to minimize the impact of such biases on their ultimate conclusions. Their process of interpretation includes the analysis not only of the details individually but also the determination of whether the details collectively constitute evidence in favor of a position that could withstand careful scrutiny. When alternative sets of evidence exist, they systematically compare and contrast the relative strength of the arguments to determine which sets cannot be eliminated at the present time. When they face a situation that mandates the formulation of action plans, they use the results of their analyses to evaluate the pros and the cons of the options before their decision as to the most appropriate course(s) of action.

ASDDFFEHTGKL
SDKHFUNERGN
MSDREADSQNN
SDGSJTUMUTJ
LKBETWEENUK
WJEWFASKSDJ
USMOTHEDAJD
SQSAKJDDHBD
GDGLINESDVB
ROPQWEOPZDN
JOSWERBRTERV
VRGTRUTUTRHG

SECTION 4: INTEGRATION

The dimension of "integration" references how a clinical student or a clinical practitioner constructs a uniform picture from disparate information collected from diverse sources. To integrate information, critical thinkers, after comparing and contrasting the information they have collected, reveal themes apparent across the collection of details and weave those themes into a model for a process or a phenomenon. As critical thinkers integrate, they start with the foundational knowledge they accumulated before their encounter with the task at hand, then assimilate and accommodate with respect to that knowledge. With respect to assimilation, critical thinkers relate "new" information to "old" information from their experiences and expertise and thus expand their existing knowledge base. With respect to accommodation, critical thinkers expand and edit their knowledge base to coalesce "new" with "old" information with the resolution of apparent discrepancies between the two with the identification of the common elements at their core. More than a summary of separate sources of infor-

mation, an integration represents interwoven details that critical thinkers may interpret in ways distinctive from previous presentations. To integrate information, critical thinkers step away from their personal orientations and insert themselves into the perspectives of the sources of the information they have collected to determine the intention of the producers and not simply the interpretation of the consumers of these details. At the conclusion of integration, critical thinkers are poised to formulate appropriate recommendations for future directions in inquiry to further expand a knowledge base, to resolve disputes and discrepancies that continue to exist with respect to the model that they have formulated, and/or to test potential applications of their ideas for new audiences, new circumstances, or—for SLPs—new clinical needs.

SECTION 5: INTENTIONALITY

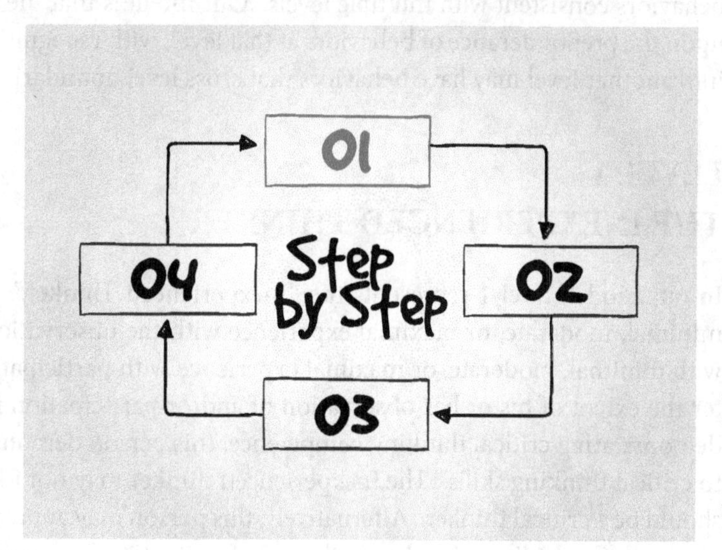

© Shutterstock/dizain

The dimension of "intentionality" references how a clinical student or a clinical practitioner systematically presents his or her response to a critical thinking task, with the implication that the intentionality of the product is correlated with the intentionality of the process. No matter the modality of the presentation of their responses, critical thinkers frame these responses within an identifiable macrostructure. Several variations of macrostructure exist: spatial, in which one provides a series of conclusions, each followed by the evidence to support that conclusion; temporal, in which one describes a process from commencement to conclusion; topical, in which one provides overviews of selected topics (which may be superficially or substantively related); cause-effect, in which one presents a situation, then describes the factors that cause or contribute to that particular situation; problem-solution, in which one presents a condition, then analyzes potential solutions to that problem; and comparative, in which one compares and contrasts the approaches to one or more dimensions of the critical thinking task at hand. No matter which macrostructures critical thinkers select, what remains constant is the logic of their response to the critical thinking task and, based upon that logic, the construction of an argument(s) that their audience can comprehend, then critique and decide whether to accept. To enhance the intentionality of their responses, critical thinkers employ appropriate microstructures. Microstructure, which employs various linguistic cohesion devices, allows critical thinkers to relate sections of their macrostructures to each other in additive, contrastive, subtractive, or other means and to link each individual proposition to the macrostructure overall. Taken as a whole, the macrostructure and microstructure allow critical thinkers to demonstrate to their audiences the clarity and ultimately the success of their thinking processes.

SECTION 6: LEVELS

Now that we have described the areas that we consider important to evaluate, we will continue with a description of the levels of competence that we apply to these areas as we determine the sophistication of the critical thinking that a clinical student or a clinical practitioner has demonstrated in a task (which we will describe in a subsequent section).

In the creation of these levels, we have promoted the idea that critical thinking can increase in sophistication. We believe that, with a system such as ours, an evaluator can capture the level of performance in response to an evaluation or an intervention scenario. Rather than ask an evaluator to discern minute gradations that differentiate one level, we have chosen to include four broad, relatively easily discernible levels of observable skill. We acknowledge that individuals will rarely demonstrate skills that are entirely confined to one level. Across the areas of information, innovation, interpretation, integration, and intentionality, levels may vary. Additionally, even within one area—information, for instance—an individual may present behaviors consistent with multiple levels. Our intent is that the determination of the level of skill be based upon the preponderance of behaviors at that level, with recognition that an individual transitioning from or into another level may have behaviors that cross level boundaries.

LEVEL 1
THE INEXPERIENCED THINKER

In our model, level 1 represents the "Inexperienced Thinker." The inexperienced thinker may have had minimal, moderate, or maximal experience with the observation of critical thinking scenarios, combined with minimal, moderate, or maximal experience with participation in critical thinking scenarios. No matter the extent of his or her observation of and/or participation in scenarios that provide opportunities for demonstrating critical thinking competence, this person demonstrates minimal sophistication with respect to critical thinking skills. The inexperienced thinker may not identify a situation as one in which he or she should be a critical thinker. Alternatively, this person may appreciate that critical thinking would be the best approach for dealing with the challenges of a situation but simply may not know how to start and/or proceed to complete the task at hand. The inexperienced thinker may randomly attempt to answer a question, resolve a dilemma, or pursue a solution, but may neither understand the rationale for the selected approach nor appreciate how to evaluate whether his or her particular approach has been successful. For the inexperienced thinker, the focus is on the attempt, not on the systematic move toward a desired end.

LEVEL 2
THE IMITATIVE THINKER

In our model, level 2 represents the "Imitative Thinker." The imitative thinker has had some level of experience with the observation of and/or participation in critical thinking scenarios. This person identifies situations in which he or she should be a critical thinker, and both appreciates the connections between elements of situations (for instance, that questions need answers, dilemmas need resolutions, and problems need solutions) and realizes that some form(s) of critical thinking are essential to move from the commencements to the conclusions of situations. With that said, however, the imitative thinker approaches situations in a formulaic manner. In some cases, he or she approaches situations in the same fashion as those observed have performed and without appreciation for the theoretical foundations of the methods employed. In some cases, this person also implements protocols established for specific contexts (for instance, a protocol described in a manual for a specific clinical procedure) without familiarity with the viable alternatives and the reason that a specific one is preferred for a particular context. In such cases, the end result becomes completion of the steps of the process rather than attainment of an end result.

LEVEL 3
THE INQUISITIVE THINKER

In our model, level 3 represents the "Inquisitive Thinker." The inquisitive thinker has typically a moderate or maximal level of experience with the observation of and participation in critical thinking scenarios. This person identifies situations in which he or she should be a critical thinker and, in fact, approaches the majority of situations with this mindset. The inquisitive thinker appreciates the connections between elements of situations and the value of critical thinking for moving from commencement to conclusion within these situations. Rather than follow a script or a routine for a context, however, the inquisitive thinker frames that context in terms of what he or she must accomplish (i.e., what questions should be answered, what dilemmas should be resolved, or what problems should be solved), accompanied by what procedures would best serve to reach a desired end. At each step of the process of critical thinking, the inquisitive thinker reflects his or her progress thus far, then uses this self-monitoring to inform any necessary self-correcting to enhance the critical thinking further. This person focuses on both the process and the product and, while using proven strategies, still individualizes his or her critical thinking to the specific task at hand.

LEVEL 4
THE INGENIOUS THINKER

In our model, level 4 represents the "Ingenious Thinker." The ingenious thinker has typically a maximal level of experience with the observation of and participation in critical thinking scenarios and approaches the majority of situations with a critical thinking mindset. He or she appreciates the connections—whether visible or invisible—between elements of situations and the value of critical thinking for addressing each element within a situation. The ingenious thinker ascertains every possible need to be addressed, as well as every possible outcome, within a situation, as well as formulates and evaluates every possible course of action, both separately and in relation to every other possibility. The ingenious thinker uses self-monitoring and self-correcting to enhance his or her critical thinking further at each step, from commencement to conclusion, within a situation. This person implements a wide variety of critical thinking strategies from both personal and non-personal sources that are relevant to the specific task at hand. Rather than retain a focus on the present task, however, the ingenious thinker relates needs within this task to elements of other critical thinking situations that he or she has observed, completed, or learned about, even when the connections across those situations are not readily apparent to one who thinks in a more superficial fashion.

SECTION 7: INSTRUCTIONS

The instructions that follow are those we have presented to participants in critical thinking tasks that we have devised to evaluate our critical thinking tool in the process of its creation.

Step 1. Become well versed in the definitions of the dimensions of critical thinking: Information, Innovation, Interpretation, Integration, and Intentionality.

Step 2. Become well versed in the definitions of the levels of critical thinking: The Inexperienced Thinker, The Imitative Thinker, The Inquisitive Thinker, and The Ingenious Thinker.

Step 3. Select the format of the response that the participant will provide to the prompt. The possible formats are: (a) Oral-Presentation (in which the participant responds in an oral monologue), (b) Oral-Conversation (in which the participant responds in an oral dialogue with standardized responses by the participant), (c) Written-Outline (in which the participant presents an outline of his or her response), and (d) Written-Paper (in which the participant presents a narrative of his or her response).

Step 4. Select a specific prompt from the collection of SLP evaluation and SLP intervention prompts presented later in this section.

Step 5. Present the task to the participant with standardized instructions. For Format (a), applied to the process of evaluation in clinical practice, the instructions are: "Here is a referral statement for a patient who has scheduled a SLP evaluation with you. Please describe how you will complete the process of evaluation for this specific patient." Inform the participant of the expected form that his or her response should take. For Format (a), applied to the process of intervention in clinical practice, the instructions are: "Here is a diagnostic statement for a patient who has scheduled a course of SLP intervention with you. Please describe how you will complete the process of intervention for this specific patient." Inform the participant of the expected form that his or her response should take.

For Format (b), applied to the process of evaluation in clinical practice, the instructions are: "Here is a referral statement for a patient who has scheduled a SLP evaluation with you. Please describe how you will complete the process of evaluation for this specific patient. I will present questions to you on a periodic basis. When you have presented the complete amount of information that you want to share, please indicate this, and we will conclude our conversation." Inform the participant of the expected form that his or her response should take. For Format (b), applied to the process of intervention in clinical practice, the instructions are: "Here is a diagnostic statement for a patient who has scheduled a course of SLP intervention with you. Please describe how you will complete the process of intervention for this specific patient." Inform the participant of the expected form that his or her response should take.

For Format (c), applied to the process of evaluation in clinical practice, the instructions are: "Here is a referral statement for a patient who has scheduled a SLP evaluation with you. Please create an annotated outline of how you will complete the process of evaluation for this specific patient." Inform the participant of the expected form that his or her response should take. For Format (c), applied to the process of intervention in clinical practice, the instructions are: "Here is a diagnostic statement for a patient who has scheduled a course of SLP intervention with you. Please create an annotated outline of how you will complete the process of evaluation for this specific patient." Inform the participant of the expected form that his or her response should take.

For Format (d), applied to the process of evaluation in clinical practice, the instructions are: "Here is a referral statement for a patient who has scheduled a SLP evaluation with you. Please describe how you will complete the process of evaluation for this specific patient." For Format (d), applied to the process of intervention in clinical practice, the instructions are: "Here is a diagnostic statement for a patient who has scheduled a course of SLP intervention with you. Please describe how you will complete the process of evaluation for this specific patient."

Please Note: Should the prompt to be presented to the participant relate to an evaluation-related or intervention-related clinical issue, the instructions are adapted to state, "Here is a clinical issue related to the process of SLP evaluation," or "Here is a clinical issue related to the process of SLP intervention," followed by the remainder of the instruction present above, with "clinical issue" inserted for "evaluation" or "intervention" as needed.

Step 6. Document the response of the participant. For oral administration of the critical thinking task, the evaluator may record, then transcribe a verbatim record of the responses of the participant. As an alternative, the evaluator may match each dimension of critical thinking to a level of critical thinking skill in real time as the participant provides his or her responses. For written administration of the critical thinking task, the evaluator will receive a document comprised of either an outline or a narrative of information in response to the prompt.

Step 7. Evaluate the response of the participant. Match each dimension of critical thinking—Information, Innovation, Interpretation, Integration, Intentionality—to the level that best represents the level of sophistication the participant demonstrates for that dimension. Please Note: The response of a participant may reflect multiple levels of critical thinking within one particular dimension. For instance, within the "Information" dimension, a participant may offer a response that reflects elements of two or three different levels (as an example). When this is the case, the level of sophistication awarded to the participant is based on the preponderance of the evidence. That is, the level awarded is the one most frequently represented in the response. The evaluator awards a score to each dimension of critical thinker based on the level of sophistication the participant demonstrates for that dimension. The level of "Inexperienced Thinker" is worth 1 point, while the level of "Imitative Thinker" is worth 2 points. The level of "Inquisitive Thinker" is worth 3 points, while the level of "Ingenious Thinker" is worth 4 points. In our tool, therefore, a participant may earn a maximum of 20 points.

Step 8. Interpret the response of the participant. Based upon the pattern of the levels of critical thinking across the dimensions of critical thinking, the evaluator and the participant can create a professional development plan to advance the development of critical thinking in the participant.

LEVEL 1 The Inexperienced Thinker

Information	-- The thinker is not familiar with the scholarly literature of the discipline in terms of sources, themes, conceptual frameworks, research methods, and/or controversies. -- The thinker is not familiar with the clinical practice standards of the discipline in terms of code of ethics, scope of practice, professional credentials, relevant laws, and/or institutional rules. -- The thinker has not mastered the scientific theories and factual information that constitute the foundations of clinical research and clinical practice in the discipline. -- The thinker has not mastered the competencies related to appropriate clinical service delivery in terms of prevention, evaluation, intervention, and consultation for patients and their families. -- The thinker primarily relies on emotion and/or opinion and considers internal (that is, his/her own perspective) factors rather than external factors as authoritative sources of information.
Innovation	-- When faced with an evaluation or treatment scenario, the thinker has minimal, if any, ideas as to how to attempt to address the situation and relies on prompts from others to even start the attempt. -- When faced with an evaluation or treatment scenario, the thinker attempts to address the situation but presents inappropriate potential solutions that focus on individual aspects of the scenario.
Interpretation	-- As he/she addresses evaluation and treatment scenarios, the thinker presents ideas and information but does not critique their accuracy, relevance, validity, or theoretical foundations. -- As he/she encounters ideas, the thinker does not systematically evaluate the pros and the cons of them, nor does he/she employ a system to rank-order these ideas on an appropriate continuum.
Integration	-- The thinker collects, retains, and retrieves information in a compartmentalized fashion. -- The thinker cannot identify principles or themes that are present across various pieces of information and does not relate individual pieces of information to an identifiable framework.
Intentionality	-- The thinker addresses an evaluation or treatment scenario in a reactionary fashion. Little or no evidence of logical, sequential thinking exists. -- No identifiable macro-structure exists in oral or written narratives in which the thinker describes his/her approach to a clinical scenario.

LEVEL 2 The Imitative Thinker

Information	-- The thinker has limited familiarity with the scholarly literature of the discipline in terms of sources, themes, conceptual frameworks, research methods, and/or controversies. He/she focuses on the scholarly literature considered important by his/her mentors or clinical practice site. -- The thinker has limited familiarity with the clinical practice standards of the discipline in terms of code of ethics, scope of practice, professional credentials, relevant laws, and/or institutional rules. He/she focuses on the policies and procedures in place at his/her clinical practice site. -- The thinker has limited mastery of the scientific theories and factual information that constitute the foundations of clinical research and clinical practice in the discipline. He/she borrows from multiple scientific theories to form his/her own, even when their precepts are contradictory. -- The thinker has limited mastery of the competencies related to appropriate clinical service delivery in terms of prevention, evaluation, intervention, and consultation for patients and their families. -- The thinker primarily relies on personal experience and considers internal (that is, his/her own perspective) factors as important as external factors as authoritative sources of information. External factors are primarily those that represent the perspective of the clinical practice site.
Innovation	-- When faced with an evaluation or treatment scenario, the thinker attempts to address the situation with potential solutions that stem primarily from his/her own observations or experiences. -- When faced with an evaluation or treatment scenario, the thinker relies on established protocols, templates, scripts, or other prescribed courses of action, even when inappropriate for the scenario.
Interpretation	-- As he/she addresses evaluation and treatment scenarios, the thinker presents ideas and information but only partially critiques their accuracy, relevance, validity, or theoretical foundations. -- As he/she encounters ideas, the thinker evaluates some pros and cons of them but does so with attention to practical factors rather than philosophical or professional considerations.
Integration	-- The thinker collects, retains, and retrieves information primarily in a compartmentalized fashion but, with prompts, identifies a theme that connects some pieces of information. -- The thinker identifies a broad theme that is present within a prescribed course of action, but the theme is superficial and does not reflect the multiple relationships that exist.
Intentionality	-- The thinker addresses an evaluation or treatment scenario primarily in a reactionary fashion. However, if a scripted example of a response to a scenario exists, he/she patterns his/her approach after this particular model. -- No identifiable macro-structure exists in oral or written narratives in which the thinker describes his/her approach to a clinical scenario unless the thinker models his/her response after a scripted example with such structure.

LEVEL 3 The Inquisitive Thinker

Information	-- The thinker is familiar with the scholarly literature of the discipline in terms of sources, themes, conceptual frameworks, research methods, and/or controversies. While his/her depth and breadth of information is not comprehensive in nature, he/she has studied representative current literature. -- The thinker is familiar with the clinical practice standards of the discipline in terms of code of ethics, scope of practice, professional credentials, relevant laws, and/or institutional rules. He/she understands how these standards influence the policies/procedures of his/her clinical practice site. -- The thinker has mastered the scientific theories and factual information that constitute the foundations of clinical research and clinical practice in the discipline. He/she borrows from multiple scientific theories to form his/her own internally consistent explanations for phenomena. -- The thinker has mastered the competencies related to appropriate clinical service delivery in terms of prevention, evaluation, intervention, and consultation for patients and their families. -- The thinker primarily relies on external standards as authoritative. He/she interprets his/her own emotions and experiences within the framework provided by these external standards that professional associations and local, state, and federal entities have established.
Innovation	-- When faced with an evaluation or treatment scenario, the thinker references current clinical practice standards as the broad conceptual framework to dictate how to approach the scenario. -- When faced with an evaluation or treatment scenario, the thinker expands or modifies prescribed courses of action, with a rationale that reflects attention to the comprehensive nature of the scenario.
Interpretation	-- As he/she addresses evaluation and treatment scenarios, the thinker presents ideas and information and critiques their accuracy, relevance, validity, or theoretical foundations. -- As he/she encounters ideas, the thinker evaluates pros and cons of them with attention to both some practical factors and some philosophical or professional considerations.
Integration	-- The thinker collects, retains, and retrieves information primarily in a thematic fashion as he/she identifies multiple themes that connect pieces of information. He/she also demonstrates appreciation for the fact that information can relate to multiple themes simultaneously. -- The thinker identifies multiple broad themes that are present within both prescribed and less scripted courses of action. The thinker references both more obvious and less obvious connections across information and thus demonstrates the ability to appreciate multiple perspectives.
Intentionality	-- The thinker addresses an evaluation or treatment scenario in a logical, sequential fashion. -- An identifiable macro-structure exists in oral or written narratives in which the thinker describes his/her approach to a clinical scenario, with an introduction and a conclusion to the narrative as a whole, as well as introductions and conclusions for the sections within the narrative.

LEVEL 4 The Ingenious Thinker

Information	-- The thinker is familiar with the scholarly literature of the discipline in terms of sources, themes, conceptual frameworks, research methods, and/or controversies. His/her depth and breadth of information is comprehensive in nature. He/she identifies the themes present in the literature, as well as which collections of literature support various theoretical perspectives. He/she also critiques the quality and sufficiency of the literature and proposes directions for future scholarly inquiry. -- The thinker is familiar with the clinical practice standards of the discipline in terms of code of ethics, scope of practice, professional credentials, relevant laws, and/or institutional rules. He/she understands how these standards influence the policies/procedures of his/her clinical practice site. He/she interprets these standards in terms of their theoretical foundations and the relevant laws. -- The thinker has mastered the scientific theories and factual information that constitute the foundations of clinical research and clinical practice in the discipline. He/she borrows from multiple scientific theories to form his/her own internally consistent explanations for phenomena. He/she compares and contrasts the precepts of the relevant theories. He/she also identifies discrepancies and deficiencies in the available factual information and proposes ways to resolve these issues. -- The thinker has mastered the competencies related to appropriate clinical service delivery in terms of prevention, evaluation, intervention, and consultation for patients and their families. -- The thinker primarily relies on external standards as authoritative. He/she interprets his/her own emotions and experiences within the framework provided by these external standards that professional associations and local, state, and federal entities have established. He/she identifies the fundamental principles that underlie these external standards and render them authoritative.
Innovation	-- When faced with an evaluation or treatment scenario, the thinker references current clinical practice standards, as well as the relevant scientific theories, the literature of the discipline, and other resources to inform the course of his/her clinical service delivery. -- To the extent that such action would not invalidate them, the thinker modifies evaluation and treatment protocols in creative ways and, when appropriate protocols do not exist, creates new approaches for the collection and documentation of clinical information.
Interpretation	-- As he/she addresses evaluation and treatment scenarios, the thinker presents ideas and information from multiple interdisciplinary sources and critiques their accuracy, relevance, validity, or theoretical foundations. He/she demonstrates both inductive and deductive reasoning. -- As he/she encounters ideas, the thinker evaluates pros and cons of them with attention to practical factors and philosophical or professional considerations. The thinker also critiques potential outcomes for scenarios based upon the formulation and confirmation of clinical hypotheses.

Integration	-- The thinker collects, retains, and retrieves information in a thematic fashion as he/she identifies multiple themes that connect pieces of information. He/she also demonstrates appreciation for the fact that information can relate to multiple themes simultaneously, even when the relationships across ideas are not readily apparent because of their level of abstraction. -- The thinker identifies multiple broad themes that are present within both prescribed and less scripted courses of action. The thinker references both more obvious and less obvious connections across information and thus demonstrates the ability to appreciate multiple perspectives. He/she demonstrates a depth and breadth of information from interdisciplinary sources.
Intentionality	-- The thinker addresses an evaluation or treatment scenario in a logical, sequential fashion, both within the sections of the narrative and across the narrative as a whole. -- An identifiable macro-structure exists in oral or written narratives in which the thinker describes his/her approach to a clinical scenario, with an introduction and a conclusion to the narrative as a whole, as well as introductions and conclusions for the sections within the narrative. The thinker complements the macro-structure with appropriate transitions and cohesive devices.

CRITICAL THINKING EVALUATION MATRIX

Gunter & LeJeune (2015)

Name ____________
Score ____________

CRITICAL THINKING AREAS	CRITICAL THINKING LEVELS: LEVEL 1 I NEXPERIENCED	LEVEL 2 I MITATIVE	LEVEL 3 I NQUISITIVE	LEVEL 4 I NGENIOUS
I NFORMATION	Value = 1 Point	Value = 2 Points	Value = 3 Points	Value = 4 Points
I NNOVATION	Value = 1 Point	Value = 2 Points	Value = 3 Points	Value = 4 Points
I NTERPRETATION	Value = 1 Point	Value = 2 Points	Value = 3 Points	Value = 4 Points
I NTEGRATION	Value = 1 Point	Value = 2 Points	Value = 3 Points	Value = 4 Points
I NTENTIONALITY	Value = 1 Point	Value = 2 Points	Value = 3 Points	Value = 4 Points

SECTION 8: CRITICAL THINKING IN CLINICAL SERVICE DELIVERY: THE EVALUATION PROCESS PROMPTS

This section includes the task prompts that we have created that are related to the SLP evaluation process. We have divided the prompts into those related to three populations, pediatric, adult, and geriatric. Within each of these populations, we have then divided the prompts into those that represent potential clinical conditions presented by patients and those that reflect issues that may arise in the course of clinical service delivery. For each population, we have created 75 clinical conditions–related prompts and 25 clinical issues–related prompts, for a total of 300 prompts across the task in which you can evaluate your own critical thinking or the skills of one for whom you are a mentor.

When, in our own clinical practice, we provide SLP evaluation services for patients, we receive descriptions of the concerns either from the patients, their family members, or the professionals who have referred them to us. We also receive information about their concerns from various kinds of documentation that they forward to us: patient history forms, previous evaluation and treatment records, and referral sheets. The descriptions of the concerns which we explore can be as extensive as an entire case file or as abbreviated as capsule statements. Because of the diversity in this preliminary information, we faced a decision as to how to construct the prompts to which students and practitioners will respond in order for the evaluation of their own level of critical thinking to commence. We considered whether we should provide detailed case histories but ultimately decided that we would provide capsule statements. While less open-ended than a statement such as, "Please plan an evaluation for a patient," capsule statements, with their minimal detail that but hints at the concerns of the patient, allow the respondents to the task the most latitude in how they describe their approach to the evaluation that will allow them to reach their clinical conclusions. The prompts that follow, while not verbatim, are representative of the statements that we have received in response to the question, "What is the nature of the concern that is the basis for this SLP evaluation?" We have included representative statements from patients, their family members, and those who have referred them to us.

PEDIATRIC

Clinical Conditions

Prompt 1 (from parents). "Our child has not started to use actual words. The children in the same Parent-Child Play Group have already started to name items around them, but our child only produces various noises."

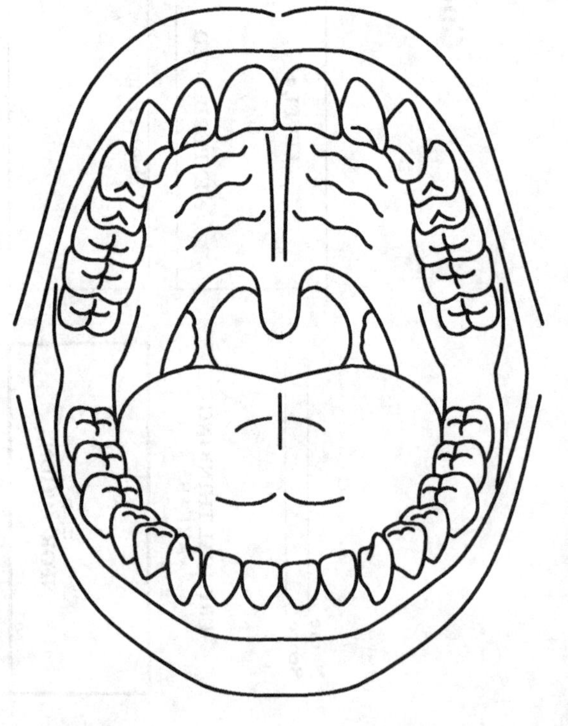

© Shutterstock/alphabetMN

Prompt 2 (from parents). "Our child does not talk nearly as much as our other two children do (older brother and older sister), and our child has not learned to communicate as well as quickly as the other two did."

Prompt 3 (from parents). "Our child understands several hundred words but uses many fewer than that. Also, our child almost always uses one or two words at a time and does not combine them into complete sentences."

Prompt 4 (from teacher). "The student confuses words that are similar in what they mean (for instance, the names of animals or clothes). Because of this, the child needs frequent correction related to his/her vocabulary."

Prompt 5 (from teacher). "The student cannot easily recall words. This occurs when he/she is asked directly to name items, as well as when he/she presents information to the class, such as in reports about selected topics."

Prompt 6 (from teacher). "The student needs multiple repetitions of information. He/she appears to find it hard to relate individual pieces of information to each other, as well as to express many ideas clearly and correctly."

Prompt 7 (from parents). "Our child leaves the ends off words. When he/she wants a cookie, he/she says 'cookie' but reaches for more after we only share one. Why can't our child add the ends to words to let us know?"

Prompt 8 (from parents). "Our child still uses words like 'mooses' and 'mouses' instead of the words the other children use. It can be cute, but we have started to become concerned. Why does our child still use these?"

Prompt 9 (from parents). "When our child produces sentences, these often don't make sense. It is like our child moves the words around so that they are not in the proper order. The words are combined but not correctly."

Prompt 10 (from teacher). "The student struggles with grammar in the language arts classes, with many errors in writing various kinds of sentences. These have many grammatical errors, such as noun-verb disagreement."

Prompt 11 (from teacher). "The other children who are grouped with this student find it hard to follow the instructions he/she provides for how to complete something, and this student finds it hard to understand others."

Prompt 12 (from teacher). "When the student attempts to tell stories (as in book reports or t.v. show descriptions), the stories are very hard to follow, with lots of backing up, starting over, and repeating information."

Prompt 13 (from physician). "The patient presented with minimal affect, minimal eye contact, and minimal one- to two-word non-informative responses to questions, as well, and needed multiple prompts to add details."

Prompt 14 (from physician). "The patient reported considerable reluctance to interact with others and indicated that he/she preferred to play or work alone rather than with other children at school or in the home."

Prompt 15 (from physician). "The patient echoed each physician comment verbatim in response to both comments and questions and presented with evidence of self-injurious behaviors such as chewing his/her fingers."

Prompt 16 (from teacher). "The student finds it hard to read the words in even the lowest level books. He/she knows some one-syllable words when he/she sees them but cannot sound out the multi-syllabic words."

Prompt 17 (from teacher). "Most students in the class—but not this student—can have fun with their words (such as in rhyming, moving sounds around, building words from sounds, or breaking words down into sounds).

Prompt 18 (from teacher). "This student seems not to appreciate humor. He/she does not understand the jokes and riddles of the other children and also does not realize when they are sarcastic or non-literal in some way."

Prompt 19 (from physician). "The patient refuses to speak except to stuffed animals and only speaks to those toys in the privacy of his/her bedroom with the door closed. The patient will not speak in the presence of people."

Prompt 20 (from physician). "The patient presents with unintelligible speech. The parents report that they understand 25%, that familiar individuals understand 15%, and that unfamiliar individuals understand 5% or less."

Prompt 21 (from physician). "In the course of the visit, the patient mispronounced many words that children at the same developmental level would find easy to say. These were typically multi-syllable complicated words."

Prompt 22 (from other SLP). "The child presented with errors related to multiple phonemes. The phonemes were unrelated in terms of their phonetic features (manner-place-voice) and included both vowels and consonants."

Prompt 23 (from other SLP). "The child presented with what the parents called a 'lisp' but had phoneme production errors in addition to those that typically affect the phonemes most frequently affected by a lisp."

Prompt 24 (from other SLP). "The child presented with errors related to specific phoneme classes. Affected places of production were alveolar and palatal, while affected manners of production were fricatives and affricates."

Prompt 25 (from parents). "Our child has very inconsistent speech errors in words. Some days he/she says a word entirely correctly, but then some other days he/she says one (or more) sounds in the word incorrectly."

Prompt 26 (from parents). "When our child tries to say more complicated words—like those with four or five syllables—he/she often places the emphasis on the incorrect syllable. The words sound peculiar because of this."

Prompt 27 (from parents). "When our child makes an error with a sound, we say it and ask him/her to say it after us. However, our child cannot imitate the sound correctly, even when we provide hints about what to do."

Prompt 28 (from other SLP). "The child presented with intact structure and function of the speech production mechanism but also with what appeared to be multiple speech sound errors that were habitual in nature."

Prompt 29 (from other SLP). "The child presented with what appeared to be fossilized speech sound production errors that were resistant to the effects of extended periods of therapy with many different approaches."

Prompt 30 (from other SLP). "The child inserts 'noises' into his/her speech that resemble the compensatory behaviors produced by children with craniofacial anomalies, velar insufficiency, or non-fluency. Please evaluate."

Prompt 31 (from parents). "Both the teacher and the physician for our child have mentioned the possibility of Childhood Apraxia of Speech to explain the patterns in our child's speech. Is this the actual condition our child has?"

Prompt 32 (from parents). "Our child has speech that we would describe as 'broken,' with many sounds deleted to the point that some words only consist of one sound. Plus, the child actually knows very few sounds."

Prompt 33 (from parents). "We are very concerned for our child. The other children at school tease him/her because of his/her speech. The child is now very self-conscious and embarrassed when he/she attends therapy."

Prompt 34 (from physician). "The patient presented with cerebral palsy from birth. Speech was characterized by inconsistent loudness, weak pressure consonants, vocal harshness, hypernasal vowels, and strained movement."

Prompt 35 (from physician). "The patient experienced anoxia in the course of an accident. Speech was characterized by uncoordinated movements, slowed rate, imprecise articulation, and equalized syllable stress."

Prompt 36 (from physician). "The family reported that the patient often drooled, even when he/she had not eaten/drunk, and that his/her voice had minimal fluctuation in tone and loudness accompanied by nasal emissions."

Prompt 37 (from dentist). "The patient presented with malocclusion, as well as dental over-eruption, dental under-eruption, and supernumerary dental eruption secondary to a complete bilateral (Type 4) cleft development."

Prompt 38 (from dentist). "A dental examination revealed the presence of an apparent lack of fusion of the palatine processes covered by an intact mucosa, consistent with the characteristics of a submucous palatal cleft."

Prompt 39 (from dentist). "The patient presented with an open mouth position accompanied by an anterior lingual resting position, as well as by mild jet of the upper central incisors, mild drooling, and mild sound distortion."

Prompt 40 (from physician). "The parents reported that their child speaks very loudly. They frequently have to remind the child to speak more appropriately across situations. They worry that this could lead to voice problems."

Prompt 41 (from physician). "The parents reported that their child speaks very softly. They frequently have to remind the child to speak more appropriately across situations. They question what has led to an inaudible voice."

Prompt 42 (from physician). "The parents reported that the child frequently imitated movie and television characters with unusual voices and also liked to produce unusual noises that sounded like growls, snorts, and chirps."

Prompt 43 (from teacher). "The student chronically sounded hoarse and frequently coughed and cleared his/her throat. The voice sounded better at the start of the day than at the end, when it became very hard to hear."

Prompt 44 (from teacher). "The student perpetually sounded as if he/she had a cold. However, the student rarely had coughing, nose-blowing, draining, or other symptoms that would suggest seasonal allergies or illnesses."

Prompt 45 (from teacher). "Other students tease this student about his/her voice because, when he/she talks, the voice sounds like a 'snort' at some points, and the child also appears to have some moisture come from the nose."

Prompt 46 (from SLP). "The parents reported frequent hesitations and repetitions in the speech of the child, which fluctuated across situations and appeared more often when the child attempted to produce complex sentences."

Prompt 47 (from SLP). "The child produced part-word repetitions in word initial position and whole-word repetitions, as well as interjections of 'like' and 'okay' into his/her speech and diminished eye contact with listeners."

Prompt 48 (from SLP). "The child reported that he/she was very scared to present reports and speeches to other students and that he/she did not like to talk on the phone unless the call was absolutely necessary for safety."

Prompt 49 (from teacher). "The child talks very quickly no matter what the situation—recess, team work, lunch, art/music. When others ask him/her to slow down, he/she does but then becomes fast after a short time."

Prompt 50 (from teacher). "The child talks very slowly. Sometimes it appears like he/she is thinking about what he/she should say, but other times it appears like he/she knows what to say but is having trouble saying it fast."

Prompt 51 (from teacher). "When the child tries to say words that are unfamiliar or complicated (such as those with multiple syllables), the child's speech is unusual, with stress on the incorrect syllable or on every one."

Prompt 52 (from physician). "The child experienced fall at school four hours prior and complained of blurred vision. The parents reported their observations of clumsiness, slurred speech, and apparent confusion in the child."

Prompt 53 (from physician). "The child presented with altered behavior subsequent to a MVA 24 hours prior and complained of being 'tired' and that lights and sounds 'hurt to be around.' Child also reported 'feeling queasy.'"

Prompt 54 (from physician). "The child presented with a history of frequent (2-3 times/day) episodes of 'staring into space' accompanied by a reported decrease in attention to and successful mastery of academic material."

Prompt 55 (from physician). "The child presented with a history of episodes of drooling, grunting, shaking, teeth clenching, and clothes picking, before which the child reported nausea and flashing lights in his/her sight."

Prompt 56 (from physician). "The parents reported that the child had a severe headache, accompanied by nausea and vomiting, mild unilateral muscle weakness, and slurred speech since his/her arrival home from school."

Prompt 57 (from physician). "After he received a forceful tackle in football, the patient experienced severe headache, accompanied by 14 hours of continuous sleep and the inability to stand without the support of furniture."

Prompt 58 (from audiologist). "A newborn infant hearing screening identified the patient as at-risk for hearing loss from maternal rubella. The patient did not respond to moderately loud environmental auditory stimuli."

Prompt 59 (from audiologist). "The patient presented with severe bilateral sensorineural hearing loss accompanied by reduced speech production accuracy and reduced comprehension of sound-based information."

Prompt 60 (from audiologist). "The patient presented with a history of frequent otitis media, which resulted in the placement of pressure equalization tubes bilaterally on three occasions and the need for later tympanoplasty."

Prompt 61 (from parent). "Our child does not hear us when he/she is in another room. When we come into the room where the child is, he/she still needs to look directly at us and, even then, does not always understand."

Prompt 62 (from parent). "Our child has attended therapy for over two years and only says approximately 10 words clearly. We want to explore the options in the event that our child never has an extensive amount of speech."

Prompt 63 (from parent). "Several children at the school our child attends have communication devices. We are curious to know whether some of these kinds of devices would be appropriate for our child to learn to use."

Prompt 64 (from parent). "Our child currently uses a high-tech augmentative communication system. We wonder whether this is the best possible system to enable our child to communicate as effectively as he/she can."

Prompt 65 (from parent). "Our child prefers to use signs over speech to communicate. We are concerned about whether this could negatively impact the speech development of our child and are not sure how to respond."

Prompt 66 (from parent). "We are introducing our child to both our languages—Spanish and French—as well as to English (which is our second language). The child has now stopped talking altogether, and we are concerned."

Prompt 67 (from parent). "Our child is learning two languages simultaneously but appears to be much stronger in one language than in the other. We are concerned that our child may have some kind of language issue."

Prompt 68 (from parent). "We want our child to learn as many languages as possible, but we are not sure how to introduce languages to him/her . . . and we are not even sure that our child has the skill to learn more than one."

Prompt 69 (from parent). "Our child has been teased by other children in his/her class, who have noted that he/she speaks 'differently' from them. We moved to this area two years ago from another region of the country."

Prompt 70 (from psychologist). "The student presented difficulties with the manual formulation of print and cursive letters, which resulted in handwriting that was often illegible. The student switched between his/her hands."

Prompt 71 (from psychologist). "The student produced written narrative papers with no easily identifiable macro-structure and which were characterized by 'stream of consciousness' content rather than systematic form."

Prompt 72 (from psychologist). "The student presented difficulties with the comprehension and interpretation of written passages in that he/she could neither paraphrase nor answer factual or speculative questions about them."

Prompt 73 (from physician). "The child presented with preferences for food textures and colors, with frequent refusal to attempt to eat other foods and frequent expulsion of other foods from his/her mouth when fed them."

Prompt 74 (from physician). "The child presented with gagging, choking, and regurgitating related to food, as well as substantial secretions during feeding. The child had frequent upper respiratory infections and congestion."

Prompt 75 (from physician). "The child experienced failure to thrive, accompanied by sleeplessness and suspected sleep apnea, as well as a bluish tint to his/her skin, suspected dehydration, and frequent crying/fussing."

PEDIATRIC

Clinical Issues

Prompt 1. The parents of the child have unusual explanations for the causes of communication disorders, which resemble folklore (for instance, the idea that nutritional patterns or specific vaccines cause such disorders).

Prompt 2. The parents of the child insist that the SLP provide a clear, comprehensive explanation for the cause of the communication disorder their child presents so that the cause can inform the course of the treatment.

Prompt 3. Prior to the time of the appointment, the parents of the child request that you include specific procedures in the evaluation, such as administer specific norm-referenced tests or conduct specific sample analyses.

Prompt 4. The parents indicate that their desire in the evaluation is that you, the SLP, collect evidence to support a specific diagnosis of a communication disorder for one or more reasons they consider very important.

Prompt 5. The parents of the child, even after explanations, misinterpret norm-referenced test scores that a child earned in an evaluation as they confuse scores with each other or confuse names of scores with similar terms.

Prompt 6. The parents of the child, even after explanations, do not understand the differences across similar conditions or disorders and thus use inappropriate labels for the pattern of communication their child presents.

Prompt 7. The parents of the child are unclear as to why specific clinical tools are included in the evaluation of their child in terms of the purpose, procedures, potential results and pros/cons are for specific clinical tools/tasks.

Prompt 8.The parents of the child, even after explanations, are unclear as to the nature of a specific diagnosis for a communication disorder and how that diagnosis stems from evaluation results and leads to recommendations.

Prompt 9. The parents of the child have received a diagnosis from another SLP. They disagree with that particular diagnosis and have scheduled an evaluation with you to obtain a second opinion related to the condition.

Prompt 10. The parents of the child have received a diagnosis from another SLP. After your evaluation, you discover that you disagree with the original diagnosis and must present the rationale for your view to the parents.

Prompt 11. The parents of the child have received multiple diagnoses for the communication disorder their child presents. They have become confused about the reason(s) for such variation in the conclusions of evaluators.

Prompt 12. After your evaluation, you, the SLP, provide the parents with a diagnosis for their child. The parents disagree with your diagnosis and attempt to argue with you that their interpretation is the correct diagnosis.

Prompt 13. After you present your diagnosis to the parents of a child, they disagree with each other as to whether to accept this as an accurate conclusion, and each parent pressures you, the SLP, to affirm/alter your view.

Prompt 14. You believe that information from consultations with other professionals would be helpful in the evaluation process. However, the parents of the child have not complied with your request that they pursue these.

Prompt 15. You believe that information from prior documentation of clinical services (evaluation and treatment) from other professionals would be helpful, but the parents refuse permission for you to receive this.

Prompt 16. After your evaluation, the parents of the child insist that your report include specific information related to your descriptions of the behavior of the child and your provision of the test scores and analysis results.

Prompt 17. After your evaluation, the parents of the child insist that your report include specific recommendations that will increase the likelihood that the child will/will not receive certain professional services.

Prompt 18. After your evaluation, you present what you consider appropriate recommendations (such as for reevaluation or intervention). However, the parents of the child do not intend to comply with these recommendations.

Prompt 19. The parents of the child report that they consider information from internet-based sources reliable and that they frequently visit a variety of websites to acquire information about communication and its disorders.

Prompt 20. The parents of the child name several television shows they watch and several television personalities they trust, particularly with respect to information related to how to address various clinical conditions.

Prompt 21. In the course of the evaluation, the child does not consistently demonstrate compliance with the clinical procedures as seen in his/her responses to your requests for his/her attention or performance of behaviors.

Prompt 22. Because of how the course of the evaluation unfolded, you as the SLP have reason to believe that the results of your evaluation present an overestimation of the actual level of communication skill the child possesses.

Prompt 23. Because of how the course of the evaluation unfolded, you as the SLP have reason to believe that the results of your evaluation present an underestimation of the actual level of communication skill the child possesses.

Prompt 24. In the course of your interaction with the family, because of an implicit or explicit communication or because of attitudes or actions, you become concerned that a parent(s) poses a serious threat to your welfare.

Prompt 25. In the course of your interaction with the family, you become concerned that the information literacy level of the parents is such that they cannot effectively participate in the evaluation process for their child.

ADULT

Clinical Conditions

Prompt 1 (from case worker). "The client, who resides in a minimally supervised home with seven other adults, needs effective comprehension and production of communication related to unskilled vocational activities."

Prompt 2 (from case worker). "The client presents with communication skills commensurate with those of a middle school student and interactional skills indicative of limited mastery of elements of common social routines."

Prompt 3 (from case worker). "The client demonstrates difficulty with the comprehension of words that were similar (but not identical) in what they mean, as well as substitutions of such words for each other in speech."

Prompt 4 (from human resources). "The employee uses words that are inappropriate for the situation at hand, as in the explanations of information to audiences who need more/less sophisticated vocabulary for concepts."

Prompt 5 (from human resources). "The employee has difficulty with the preparation of summaries of material, in that he/she is unable to easily identify the themes contained within the text of a variety of documents."

Prompt 6 (from human resources). "The employee finds it hard to correct his/her misinformation. Even when he/she senses the need to correct items, he/she continues to perpetuate incorrect rather than correct details."

Prompt 7 (from spouse). "My spouse has a certain kind of sound that he/she cannot produce correctly. The majority of words that contain this kind of sound are incorrect because of that, even when he/she tries very hard."

Prompt 8 (from spouse). "When my spouse says a word incorrectly, I repeat it correctly for him/her to hear, but he/she cannot easily hear the differences between what we both said. To him/her, the words sound the same."

Prompt 9 (from spouse). "Even as an adult, my spouse says words like 'deers' and 'mouses.' He/she is not very concerned about it because he/she believes that other people know what he/she means. But they comment."

Prompt 10 (from patient). "I am not always sure how to alter words correctly. For example, when I compare people, I am not sure when to say someone is 'smarter' and when someone is 'smartest' and similar kinds of choices."

Prompt 11 (from patient). "When I try to express myself, I do not always know how to phrase what I want to say. I do not think that I convey what I want to say in the most 'proper' way. It always has room for improvement."

Prompt 12 (from patient). "I find it difficult to provide instructions or directions to other people. I start, then I move ahead with information, and then I have to back up because I realize that I need to add some more details."

Prompt 13 (from human resources). "The employee needs improvement in interpersonal communication skills, particularly in the context of discussions with co-workers, in which the interactions are not always effective."

Prompt 14 (from human resources). "The employee must tailor his/her communication level to the nature of, topic addressed, and participants in a situation. Attention to norms for professional conduct is essential for success."

Prompt 15 (from human resources). "Co-workers comment that vocal behaviors (loud coughing, humming, throat clearing, shouting) on the part of this employee are a substantial distraction to their work in the workplace."

Prompt 16 (from physician). "The patient reported that his/her current position is in a bar with considerable tobacco smoke and which involves talking for extended periods and over noise, with little time for water breaks."

Prompt 17 (from physician). "The patient presented with a history of multiple episodes of acute laryngitis resulting from intermittent vocal abuse, which now presented as chronic laryngitis in the absence of vocal overuse."

Prompt 18 (from physician). "The patient presented with vocal fry and harshness. He/she reported that his/her vocal quality diminishes from the start of the day to the end, with faster decline with increased voice use."

Prompt 19 (from spouse). "My spouse has an unusual voice. It is somewhat lower pitched than it used to be. And sometimes it sounds as if he/she speaks in a whisper, even when a normal loudness level is his/her intention."

Prompt 20 (from spouse). "My spouse always sounds out of breath when he/she talks, even when he/she hasn't been working out, walking fast, or working hard. He/she strains to not sound so out of breath but to no avail."

Prompt 21 (from spouse). "My spouse sounds as if he/she has a cold, even when he/she does not. Several of our friends ask me if he/she has been sick recently, but his/her voice sounds this way even outside allergy season."

Prompt 22 (from patient). "My friends often ask me where I am from. They tell me that my voice sounds 'nasal.' I have never lived in a place where people talk with a nasal voice. But I know that others think that I have."

Prompt 23 (from patient). "When I call people who do not know me on the telephone, they frequently talk to me like I am a child because of how my voice sounds. They are often surprised when they learn that I am an adult."

Prompt 24 (from patient). "My friends tell me that I do not sound like my sex, that my voice is too (high pitched/low pitched) for a (man/woman). They sometimes ask me if I intentionally try to sound like the other sex."

Prompt 25 (from human resources). "The employee speaks very loudly while he/she is on the phone, a participant in discussions, in the lunch area, and a participant in conversations. Fellow employees are distracted."

Prompt 26 (from human resources). "In both professional and personal interactions, other employees report that this particular employee is very hard to hear and that they frequently ask him/her to 'speak up' in order to hear."

Prompt 27 (from human resources). "The employee experiences unusual incidents with his/her voice of sufficient frequency that co-workers and supervisors have noticed them. The voice shifts in its pitch dramatically."

Prompt 28 (from spouse). "My spouse sometimes becomes louder, then softer, then louder when he/she speaks. I asked if he/she means to be funny, but he/she says this is definitely not intentional, but is unexpected."

Prompt 29 (from spouse). "As a child, my spouse had speech therapy at school. However, there is one sound that he/she still cannot easily say. I don't know if this was never completely corrected or if he/she has relapsed."

Prompt 30 (from spouse). "My spouse does not say many of his/her sounds correctly, so many words he/she says are incorrect. I know that he/she is very sensitive to this, especially at work and when we meet new people."

Prompt 31 (from patient). "I have discovered that I cannot easily pronounce many words. It is not that the words are that difficult. I just need several attempts at practice before I can say them the way that others say them."

Prompt 32 (from patient). "I have started to take some classes so that I can advance professionally, and a lot of the technical words in my textbooks are very hard for me to pronounce. I wish that I could more easily say them."

Prompt 33 (from patient). "My dentist has recommended braces for me but has warned me that any improvement in my dentition may be compromised unless I correct my swallowing and tongue resting position."

Prompt 34 (from dentist). "The patient presents with severe malocclusion (overbite) and an anterior lingual position at rest. The patient also presented with mild drooling, as well as mild oral leakage while using an oral rinse."

Prompt 35 (from dentist). "The patient communicates with speech that was difficult to understand, accompanied by bilateral facial paresis, with inability to close lips completely or extend tongue tip beyond cavity."

Prompt 36 (from dentist). "The patient speaks with a very slow rate of speech, accompanied by exaggerated movement within the jaw, as well as a vocal quality that sounded hyponasal and an inability to easily initiate speech."

Prompt 37 (from SLP). "The patient, in therapy for one year as an adult, reports participation in extensive therapy as a child, with no permanent resolution for his/her reversing, deleting, and substituting sounds in words."

Prompt 38 (from SLP). "The patient presents with characteristics consistent with apraxia of speech. He/she reported a history of two mild cerebrovascular accidents within the past six months, followed by these symptoms."

Prompt 39 (from SLP). "The patient presents with a history of stuttering characterized by initial phoneme repetitions and prolongations, frequent non-word interjections, and physical behaviors (such as clenching fists)."

Prompt 40 (from patient). "I have stuttered since I was a child. I had therapy at school, and I now participate in a local support circle for adults. I feel like my stuttering controls me, and I want to control my stuttering instead."

Prompt 41 (from patient). "When I stutter, I can't control my behavior. My eyes won't open, my mouth won't close, and my hands and feet twitch. I turn red and start to sweat. I want very much for these behaviors to stop."

Prompt 42 (from patient). "Some situations are very hard for me when I need to communicate. I tend to dread them and avoid them if I can. I know that I need to know how to handle these situations much more effectively."

Prompt 43 (from SLP). "Across a variety of tasks involving oral reading of standardized passages, the patient produces a mean speech rate of 345 SPM. The patient reports that others frequently ask him/her to slow down."

Prompt 44 (from SLP). "The patient produces speech that others describe as 'slow in rate.' The patient reports that, when he/she attempts to speak more quickly, he/she is unable to do so even when he/she focuses upon this."

Prompt 45 (from SLP). "When he/she attempts to produce multi-syllabic words, the patient frequently places the emphasis upon the incorrect syllable. This pattern, when in connected speech, disrupts the rhythmic pattern."

Prompt 46 (from human resources). "The employee has an unusual speech pattern. The speech rate fluctuates from fast to slow. This is a distraction when the employee presents to our team and speaks with others."

Prompt 47 (from human resources). "The employee expressed a lack of confidence in his/her oral presentation skills, as well as his/her preference to receive duties which he/she could perform behind the scenes."

Prompt 48 (from human resources). "The supervisor has expressed concerns about the communication style of the employee, in that he/she has on occasion alienated both superiors and subordinates with his/her comments."

Prompt 49 (from audiologist). "The patient has late-onset deafness secondary to reaction to ototoxicity of drugs used in chemotherapy for cancer. The patient has a unilateral cochlear implant and limited speechreading."

Prompt 50 (from audiologist). "The patient has congenital deafness secondary to anoxia at birth. The patient is fluent in both ASL and oral/written English. The patient has started to consider the option of cochlear implant."

Prompt 51 (from audiologist). "The patient reports a history of involvement in music, which includes his/her performance in a local band for two decades as an instrumentalist (lead and bass guitars, keyboard) and a vocalist."

Prompt 52 (from physician). "The patient reports that he/she must increase the volume of the t.v. and the ratio to understand them and that he/she must move to the room where others are in order to easily understand them."

Prompt 53 (from physician). "The patient reports intermittent tingling of the extremities, as well as the onset of clumsiness, difficulty swallowing normal-sized bites or sips, and extended pauses in his/her connected speech."

Prompt 54 (from physician). "The patient presented with progressive muscle weakness, accompanied by difficulties in rising after sitting, walking and running, frequent falls, and frequent difficulty with swallowing foods."

Prompt 55 (from spouse). "My spouse presently has a high-tech communication system. He/she finds it difficult to use. We are interested in what the options would be for a better system for him/her to use at this point."

Prompt 56 (from spouse). "Ever since his/her stroke, my spouse does not communicate clearly. He/she is frustrated. However, he/she does not want to use any kind of tools, even a note pad with a pen, to convey ideas."

Prompt 57 (from spouse). "Shortly after his/her stroke, my spouse made a notable improvement in his/her communication. But, after about nine months, the improvement slowed down and now seems to have stopped."

Prompt 58 (from adult child). "My parent seems to have regressed since his/her stroke. For a while, he/she spoke relatively clearly, but now the speech seems harder to understand than ever before, even to family members."

Prompt 59 (from adult child). "My parent uses words that are not actually words. He/she thinks that what he/she says are words and becomes frustrated when the rest of us do not understand what he/she has attempted."

Prompt 60 (from adult child). "Even when we phrase what we say as simply as possible, my parent still does not understand. We have to repeat ourselves frequently and often have to use gestures to demonstrate what we say."

Prompt 61 (from spouse). "My spouse seems forgetful. He/she will have a conversation with me about a topic, then an hour later start that same conversation and not even realize that we have recently shared those comments."

Prompt 62 (from spouse). "My spouse is not the same person he/she was even this time last year. He/she becomes easily combative, and his/her communication is not as pleasant or as patient as it once was. I am worried."

Prompt 63 (from spouse). "Six months earlier, my spouse fell from a kitchen ladder onto the floor. Since then, his/her communication fluctuates, with periods in which he/she does not express even simple information clearly."

Prompt 64 (from adult child). "Since a serious motor vehicle accident one year earlier, my parent uses a wheelchair for mobility and a variety of simple ways to communicate (such as gesturing or writing notes on cards)."

Prompt 65 (from adult child). "My parent was the victim of a brutal assault. His/her demeanor is very different now, as he/she is reserved and withdrawn and, for the most part, uncommunicative with his/her children."

Prompt 66 (from adult child). "After my parent fell while mountain climbing, he/she appears confused about how to perform relatively simple tasks. However, he/she denies that we have any reason to be concerned with this."

Prompt 67 (from patient). "I had my larynx removed because of cancer. I have tried to learn to use esophageal speech, but I have not found it easy. I still sound very breathy because I cannot vibrate all of the air that I swallow."

Prompt 68 (from patient). "Before I have my laryngectomy I want to find out how I will be able to communicate right afterwards and how long I will have to wait before I have a normal sounding voice once again."

Prompt 69 (from patient). "I want to improve how well I can use my speech valve to communicate. I am still not satisfied with how my speech sounds, and I think that I can do better. Maybe I should try a different valve."

Prompt 70 (from physician). "The patient presents with difficulties with swallowing, secondary to a tracheostomy. The patient also needs speech valve trials to enable him/her to speak as soon as he/she safely can."

Prompt 71 (from physician). "The patient presents with penetration and aspiration of liquids and solids, accompanied by pockets of bolus in the cheeks and weakness in the attempt to clear the bolus from the oral cavity."

Prompt 72 (from physician). "The patient presents with the inability to form a lip seal, accompanied by leak both of liquids and solids from the oral cavity, as well as by the inability to intake sips and bites of appropriate sizes."

Prompt 73 (from spouse). "My spouse has many problems with food. He/she frequently coughs after eating or drinking and then complains that food is 'stuck' in his/her throat. Some textures and thicknesses are a challenge."

Prompt 74 (from spouse). "My spouse was born in another country. He/she learned English at school as a second language. Our friends here can hear that he/she has accented English that is sometimes hard to understand."

Prompt 75 (from spouse). "We are from another part of the country, and people here notice that by how we speak. My spouse is self-conscious about how he/she sounds and would like his/her speech to be less distinctive."

ADULT

Clinical Issues

Prompt 1. The patient repeatedly questions the cause of the communication disorder you have identified and asks you to explore every aspect of his/her personal and medical history to specifically identify one or more causes.

Prompt 2. The patient asks whether some of his/her own behaviors have contributed to the presence of his/her communication disorder and may or may not accept responsibility for his/her role related to the disorder.

Prompt 3. Prior to the evaluation appointment, the patient requests that you perform specific procedures, which may or may not be relevant to your informational needs, because of his/her belief that these are valuable.

Prompt 4. At the start of the evaluation appointment, the patient indicates a desire for a specific diagnosis for a personal reason (such as to confirm/disconfirm expectations, to access clinical services, to receive claim benefits).

Prompt 5. The patient appears unclear as to the purpose of some of the evaluation tasks and questions what information such tasks contribute to the evaluation process, even after clear explanations from the SLP about them.

Prompt 6. The patient misinterprets norm-referenced scores from quantitative procedures performed in the evaluation and, because of this, reaches inaccurate conclusions about the current status of his/her communication.

Prompt 7. Because of his/her literacy level, the patient does not comprehend the evaluation report prepared by the SLP, and he/she thus files the report and does not ask the SLP to assist him/her to understand its contents.

Prompt 8. The patient reacts to certain aspects of the content of the evaluation report with requests to the SLP to remove or, as a minimum, rephrase this information for reasons such as denial, discomfort, or disappointment.

Prompt 9. The patient provides inaccurate history information, unintentionally, which leads to underestimation and/or overestimation of his/her current level and an inaccurate clinical hypothesis to address.

Prompt 10. The patient provides inaccurate history information, intentionally, which leads to underestimation and/or overestimation of his/her current level of skill and an inaccurate clinical hypothesis to address in the session.

Prompt 11. In response to your request that the patient set appointments with other service providers, the patient does not comply with your perception that information from them is important to the evaluation process.

Prompt 12. In response to your presentation of recommendations based upon the evaluation results and conclusions, the patient does not comply with these recommendations for reasons that he/she does not disclose.

Prompt 13. The patient disagrees with your diagnosis of a communication disorder and, in response to your diagnosis, argues with your interpretations of qualitative and quantitative information you acquired in the evaluation.

Prompt 14. The patient disagrees with specific recommendations that you made at the conclusion of the evaluation and requests that you replace these recommendations with others that are more desirable to him/her.

Prompt 15. Because of what you observed in the course of the evaluation, you believe that the results of various standardized evaluation procedures presented an overestimation of the level of communication skill of the patient.

Prompt 16. Because of what you observed in the course of the evaluation, you believe that the results of various standardized evaluation procedures presented an underestimation of the level of communication skill of the patient.

Prompt 17. The patient knows (either personally or professionally) other patients whom you serve. In the course of the evaluation, he/she solicits information from you about the services you have provided to these people.

Prompt 18. At the conclusion of the evaluation, the patient refuses permission for you to forward a duplicate of the evaluation report to his/her referral source and indicates that he/she will not verbally share evaluation results.

Prompt 19. Based on the behavior of the patient in the course of the evaluation, you as the SLP conclude that you would be prudent to request a threat assessment to determine whether the patient could compromise your safety.

Prompt 20. After the evaluation, the patient frequently contacts you, the SLP, by e-mail and voice mail at both your office and your home, with increased references to personal information that you did not disclose to the patient.

Prompt 21. While the patient seriously considers your evaluation conclusions, he/she indicates that the opinions of other individuals whom he/she knows professionally are more important to him/her than your opinions.

Prompt 22. While the patient seriously considers your evaluation conclusions, he/she indicates that the opinions of other individuals whom he/she knows personally are more important to him/her than your opinions.

Prompt 23. You conduct this evaluation in response to the request from your patient for a second opinion related to his/her suspected communication disorder. You agree with the previous SLP evaluation conclusions.

Prompt 24. You conduct this evaluation in response to the request from your patient for a second opinion related to his/her suspected communication disorder. You disagree with the previous SLP evaluation conclusions.

Prompt 25. The patient presents signs that he/she is in the grieving process (such as denying, bargaining, arguing, crying, or otherwise reacting) in response to the specific communication disorder diagnosis you provide.

GERIATRIC

Clinical Conditions

Prompt 1 (from spouse). "My spouse has intermittent difficulty with following commands and producing statements. At the present, he/she understands what I say but finds it hard to name items/individuals on demand."

Prompt 2 (from spouse). "My spouse cannot easily speak or write. Recalling words is difficult for him/her, as is connecting words into sentences for explaining or describing. Attempting to speak resembles struggle at times."

© Shutterstock/Dolvalol

Prompt 3 (from spouse). "When my spouse speaks, he/she is fluent, but what he/she says is a combination of words and non-words. He/she cannot easily follow commands but often appears to believe that he/she is correct."

Prompt 4 (from case worker). "The patient presents deficits or varying degrees in both comprehension and production across spoken, written, and manual domains. The patient imitates but does not understand gestures."

Prompt 5 (from case worker). "The patient imitates monosyllabic words easily and repeats part of oral commands presented to him/her. The patient is unable to follow even one-step commands, however, or name items."

Prompt 6 (from case worker). "The patient comprehends one- and two-step commands and produces one- and two-word phrases (and imitates longer sentences). His/her writing, even his/her own name, is not legible."

Prompt 7 (from nurse). "The patient complains that he/she is unable to say what he/she wants to say. The patient replaces object names with names of related objects but produces correct names in response to descriptions."

Prompt 8 (from nurse). "The patient presents with intact auditory comprehension. The patient speaks in a fluent fashion but with substitutions of words with comparable sound or meaning but cannot always imitate words."

Prompt 9 (from nurse). "The patient easily follows one- and two-step motor commands. The patient also easily repeats three- and four-word phrases. The patient is unable to spontaneously describe familiar concrete items."

Prompt 10 (from physician). "The MRI of the right-handed patient indicates a right-hemisphere CVA. However, the patient cannot consistently follow one-step commands, easily name objects, or continuously verbalize."

Prompt 11 (from physician). "The MRI of the patient is unremarkable for cortical damage. The patient presents with mild deficits in expressive language (specifically, naming and describing) and a partial hemianopia."

Prompt 12 (from physician). "The patient non-imitatively produces monosyllable words and imitatively produces one- and two-syllable words. Automatic production is superior to non-automatic production of speech."

Prompt 13 (from spouse). "My spouse has very weak muscle movement even though his/her muscles themselves feel as if they are toned. His/her voice sounds very harsh and strident, with a noticeable nasal quality."

Prompt 14 (from spouse). "My spouse has weakness on one side of his/her face. Because of this, he/she cannot close his/her lips. When he/she attempts to speak, he/she drools, and my spouse is concerned about this."

Prompt 15 (from spouse). "When my spouse wants to speak, he/she finds it very difficult. What I can say in 1 minute takes him/her at least 2-3 minutes. He/she produces even simple words slowly with very slow movement."

Prompt 16 (from patient). "I know that I speak very quickly. Sometimes when I speak I produce grunts or other noises without intending to and without warning. My voice sounds strained, and sometimes my voice stops."

Prompt 17 (from patient). "I try to speak clearly, but I cannot always produce the sounds exactly. Sometimes I draw out my vowels even when I do not mean to. Other people tell me that I speak very slowly and imprecisely."

Prompt 18 (from patient). "I don't always remember information. People tell me that I repeat myself to them, but I don't remember these conversations that they say happened only minutes earlier. They have to remind me."

Prompt 19 (from adult child). "My parent is often unaware of where he/she is and seems surprised to learn he/she is in a certain room in the home. He/she does not even remember basic faces until we provide some cues."

Prompt 20 (from adult child). "My parent is in decline, with periods of stability then followed by periods of sudden, rapid decrease in skills. He/she can express wants and needs, then suddenly become hard to understand."

Prompt 21 (from adult child). "My parent cannot eat, bathe, or dress independently and sometimes even falls asleep before he/she has completed the task at hand. Sometimes he/she appears to hallucinate and talk to the air."

Prompt 22 (from case worker). "The patient presents with a variety of symptoms that result in management issues. These symptoms include deficits in memory, non-compliance with directions, and apparent hallucinations."

Prompt 23 (from case worker). "The patient presents with weight loss. When eating, the patient varies between fast and slow chewing, with coughing due to propulsion of food to pharynx before the start of the swallow."

Prompt 24 (from case worker). "The patient produces speech with increased rate and reduced volume. He/she can slow the speech upon request but cannot maintain the decreased rate for more than two utterances."

Prompt 25 (from spouse). "My spouse communicates less effectively with every year that passes. He/she currently has moderate problems with comprehension but severe compromise of production of more than one word."

Prompt 26 (from spouse). "My spouse speaks slowly. He/she cannot increase his/her speech rate even for very short phrases. He/she also chews food very slowly. When he/she speaks, he/she requires breaks to breathe."

Prompt 27 (from spouse). "My spouse complains of fatigue and requires a great deal of rest. His/her condition fluctuates in severity. He/she is quite forgetful. He/she always finds it hard to respond to my comments."

Prompt 28 (from physician). "The patient presents with difficulty attending to and completing tasks unless those require only a short time to complete. The spouse reports that he/she produces socially inappropriate speech."

Prompt 29 (from physician). "The patient presents with the complaint of a long-standing headache. The patient also notes the presence of memory deficits that are less severe when compared with six months previously."

Prompt 30 (from physician). "The patient lacks safety awareness. He/she overestimates his/her ability to perform home-based tasks and rationalizes errors in task completion. He/she benefits from repeated direction."

Prompt 31 (from nurse). "The patient is easily irritated. He/she argues with caregivers about the appropriateness of speech and behavior. The patient presents with memory deficits for both old and new material."

Prompt 32 (from nurse). "The patient frequently complains of pain and fatigue. The patient specifically complains that tasks that involve the application of varied cognitive skills cause him/her considerable mental fatigue."

Prompt 33 (from nurse). "The patient has reduced eye contact and reduced speech volume. He/she expresses minimal interest in eating and insists that he/she is not hungry even when presented with his/her favorite foods."

Prompt 34 (from spouse). "My spouse shows limited interest in eating. He/she sometimes wants to eat but consumes only very small amounts. His/her clothes have become very loose. He/she sleeps for most of the day."

Prompt 35 (from spouse). "My spouse needs a long time to chew food. Even after he/she takes a long time, he/she still often has food particles that remain in his/her mouth, and he/she is often not aware of these particles."

Prompt 36 (from spouse). "When he/she eats, there is no problem with chewing. However, after swallowing, his/her voice sounds 'wet.' And, when he/she coughs, food comes back into the mouth, and he/she swallows again."

Prompt 37 (from physician). "The patient swallows easily with minimal oral cavity residue. However, the patient complains of the sensation that food is 'stuck' in the area around the sternum and vomits food particles."

Prompt 38 (from physician). "The patient presents with complaints related to the swallowing process. However, results of both bedside swallow examination and modified barium swallow procedure are unremarkable."

Prompt 39 (from physician). "The patient is post-laryngectomy, with stoma, secondary to laryngeal cancer. The patient 'mouths' words but has no current ability to manipulate the respiration for voice production purposes."

Prompt 40 (from dentist). "The patient has limited lingual tissue after a partial glossectomy to treat lingual cancer. Subsequently, the patient has limited speech intelligibility and is unable to tolerate any liquid or solid intake."

Prompt 41 (from dentist). "The patient presents with only a lingual root. He/she is interested in oral intake, but presently his/her nutrition is administered via an alternative source. His/her speech intelligibility is very poor."

Prompt 42 (from dentist). "The patient is edentulous. Subsequent to this, the patient presents with a number of compensatory oral movements in speech production attempts. Speech intelligibility is substantially decreased."

Prompt 43 (from nurse). "The patient presents with reduced speech intelligibility. His/her voice is characterized by reduced loudness and breathiness. The patient expels considerable phlegm from the tracheostomy."

Prompt 44 (from nurse). "The patient attempts to imitatively and non-imitatively produce vocalization. However, no voicing is present across attempts. Audible ventilator sounds further compromise communication."

Prompt 45 (from nurse). "Subsequent to his/her recent CVA, the patient has speech characterized by slow, halting productions, accompanied by the frequent inability to produce words without an apparent physical struggle."

Prompt 46 (from psychologist). "After a near-death experience, the patient produces speech characterized by struggle behaviors and hesitations. The patient often slaps a part of his/her body to facilitate speech production."

Prompt 47 (from psychologist). "The patient presents with a decline in the quantity and quality of his/her communication with others, as well as statements that 'the world would be better without his/her presence in it.'"

Prompt 48 (from psychologist). "The family of the patient reports his/her recent, substantial decline with respect to physical, intellectual, and communication areas, as well as his/her ability to swallow even small amounts."

Prompt 49 (from SLP). "After a recent closed head injury, the patient presents with substantial inability to attend to any task. The behavior of the patient is characterized by agitation and attempts to remove his/her IV tube."

Prompt 50 (from SLP). "The patient denies that he/she has a communication disorder or any other condition in need of evaluation. He/she presents as distracted, with limited interest in interactions with family or friends."

Prompt 51 (from SLP). "The patient presents with relatively intact auditory comprehension. However, he/she is unable to recall names of items on request and affirms that he/she knows but cannot produce the names."

Prompt 52 (from spouse). "My spouse attempts to name items but, rather than produce their names, he/she talks extensively about the items with descriptions of their traits and uses. This sometimes helps with the naming."

Prompt 53 (from spouse). "When my spouse attempts to tell me the name of an item or an individual, he/she says a name that is close (such as 'pen' for 'pencil' or "Joe' for 'Joanna') but only very rarely says the same precisely."

Prompt 54 (from spouse). "My spouse attempts to name items. But, instead of actual words, he/she uses words that are not actually words that any of us knows. Then he/she acts as if he/she has named the items correctly."

Prompt 55 (from psychologist). "The patient reads aloud and accurately says the words. However, he/she does not comprehend what he/she has read and is unable to answer even simple factual questions about the text."

Prompt 56 (from psychologist). "The patient is unable to write as he/she once did. He/she has difficulty with letter formation, which results in illegible print and script. He/she also struggles with respect to what words to write."

Prompt 57 (from psychologist). "Secondary to a brain injury, the patient is unable to perform simple mathematical calculations. The patient reports that he/she is overwhelmed with checkbook account maintenance."

Prompt 58 (from patient). "I cannot sing in the church choir as I did for over twenty years. I am not able to read music nearly as easily as I once could. The notes look like dots. Also, my voice does not have much variety."

Prompt 59 (from patient). "My spouse constantly tells me that I need to brush both sides of my hair, eat foods from both sides of my plate, tie laces on shoes on both feet, and look completely around the room. I wonder why."

Prompt 60 (from patient). "My primary care physician has listed 'bipolar disorder' in my records. I do not agree with this. It is true that sometimes I hear voices in my head, but I do not consider this a cause for concern."

Prompt 61 (from spouse). "Ever since his/her stroke, we have noticed that my spouse looks straight us and does not seem to recognize us. He/she also does not know his/her favorite movie stars on television or in magazines."

Prompt 62 (from spouse). "After a recent diagnosis of anoxia during a serious cardiovascular event, my spouse requires ongoing cues and reminders to sustain his/her attention to the details of simple household chores."

Prompt 63 (from spouse). "My spouse experienced a recent closed head injury. He/she recalled distant but not recent events. He/she also continues to repeatedly ask biographical information, like our names and relations."

Prompt 64 (from adult child). "My parent seems to have lost his/her common sense. He/she violates safety precautions, and we fear he/she will have an accident. Also, he/she does not dress appropriately for the weather."

Prompt 65 (from adult child). "My parent can remember experiences from his/her childhood. Unfortunately, he/she cannot remember where he/she is today or what has happened recently even with reminders."

Prompt 66 (from adult child). "After a recent procedure, my parent uses profanity and produces inappropriate comments about individuals from minorities or with physical problems. This is entirely new behavior!"

Prompt 67 (from patient). "I do not read very well. I always had trouble reading when I was in school. I think this holds me back a lot in my life. I would love to improve my reading so that I can read my Bible every day."

Prompt 68 (from patient). "I do not write very well. I know what I want to say, but I find it very hard to find the best way to phrase it. I want write the kinds of letters to other people that they would be excited to receive."

Prompt 69 (from patient). "I do not feel comfortable when I talk in front of people. I want to be able to stand up at family reunions and say a few words, and I want to be able to stand up at church and say the prayers."

Prompt 70 (from employer). "The employee is reserved by nature and because of that does not actively participate in discussions of issues. I recommend that he/she contribute an increased quantity of valuable ideas."

Prompt 71 (from employer). "The employee works effectively in his/her specified tasks. However, he/she exhibits familiarity – sometimes excessively – in his/her varied interactions with both subordinates and superiors."

Prompt 72 (from employer). "The employee works hard but is not sufficiently attentive to details in tasks. He/she must frequently redo papers, slides, reports, and other tasks after reminders from supervisors about details."

Prompt 73 (from audiologist). "The patient reports a decrease over time in his/her ability to easily hear television or conversation. His/her spouse reports that the patient increases the television volume substantially."

Prompt 74 (from audiologist). "The patient reports that he/she experiences continuous 'ringing' in his/her ears. He also reports frequent episodes of dizziness and notes that he has needed to hold furniture for balance."

Prompt 75 (from audiologist). "The patient reports that he frequently asks his family members and friends to repeat what they say to him because he does not understand them and confuses many of their words with each other."

GERIATRIC

Clinical Issues

Prompt 1. The patient does not drive in the afternoon and expresses concerns that he/she has no family members or friends who can provide transportation to and from the clinic where the SLP evaluation is scheduled.

Prompt 2. The patient is confused about the specific services covered by his/her health insurance and the extent of the co-payment for which he/she is responsible. He/she asks whether reduced clinical fees are available.

Prompt 3. The patient demonstrates considerable resistance to the idea of an evaluation. He/she continues to insist that he/she does not present a communication disorder and does not need to participate in the evaluation.

Prompt 4. The patient is physically unable to participate in the evaluation tasks. He/she falls asleep easily, particularly when he/she sits in a chair. He/she also has diminished sight and hearing, with restricted motor skills.

Prompt 5. Prior to the evaluation appointment, the patient or spouse requests that you perform specific procedures because the professional who referred the patient for the evaluation recommended these procedures.

Prompt 6. At the start of the evaluation appointment, the patient indicates a desire for a specific diagnosis for a personal reason (such as to confirm/disconfirm expectations, to access clinical services, to receive claim benefits).

Prompt 7. The patient appears confused as to the purpose of some of the evaluation tasks and how to perform them, even after clear explanations from the SLP about them and demonstrations of sample test-related questions.

Prompt 8. The patient provides inaccurate history information because of deficits in memory, which leads to underestimation and/or overestimation of his/her current level and an inaccurate clinical hypothesis to address.

Prompt 9. In response to your request that the patient set appointments with other service providers, the patient does not or adult children do not wish to comply because they consider the appointments inconvenient.

Prompt 10. In response to your presentation of recommendations based upon the evaluation results and conclusions, the patient does not or adult children do not comply with these recommendations for unknown reasons.

Prompt 11. The patient and his/her spouse disagree with specific recommendations that you made at the conclusion of the evaluation and requests that you replace these with others that are perceived as more reasonable.

Prompt 12. The patient and his/her spouse know other patients whom you serve. They question why your conclusions and recommendations were so different from those you provided for them, who have similar concerns.

Prompt 13. While the patient seriously considers your evaluation conclusions, he/she indicates that the opinions of other individuals whom he/she knows professionally are more important to him/her than your opinions.

Prompt 14. While the patient seriously considers your evaluation conclusions, he/she indicates that the opinions of other individuals whom he/she knows personally are more important to him/her than your opinions.

Prompt 15. You conduct this evaluation in response to the request from your patient for a second opinion related to his/her suspected communication disorder. You agree with the previous SLP evaluation conclusions.

Prompt 16. You conduct this evaluation in response to the request from your patient for a second opinion related to his/her suspected communication disorder. You disagree with the previous SLP evaluation conclusions.

Prompt 17. The patient presents signs that he/she is in the grieving process (such as denying, bargaining, arguing, crying, or otherwise reacting) in response to the specific communication disorder diagnosis you provide.

Prompt 18. The patient and his/her spouse disagree with you about one or more aspects of the evaluation (such as the conclusions reached or recommendations made). They attempt to convince you to support their position.

Prompt 19. The patient and his/her spouse disagree with each other about one or more aspects of the evaluation. Each person attempts to persuade you to adopt his/her position and support you in favor of the other.

Prompt 20. The patient and his/her adult children disagree with you about one or more aspects of the evaluation. They attempt to convince you that your conclusions/recommendations are inaccurate or inappropriate.

Prompt 21. The patient and family members have extensive questions about the clinical documentation associated with the evaluation and contact you, the SLP, three times weekly for several weekly to overview these.

Prompt 22. The patient schedules this evaluation for purposes of a second opinion about a condition. You do not agree with the conclusions and recommendations of the previous service provider, and you explain your reasons.

Prompt 23. The patient schedules this evaluation for purposes of a second opinion about a condition. You find the previous conclusions and recommendations appropriate, but the patient disagrees with your specific conclusions.

Prompt 24. Confusion exists as to who is responsible for the provision of history information and authorization to distribute records, as the patient does not provide accurate details and does not understand informed consent.

Prompt 25. The spouse and/or adult children question the necessity for SLP evaluation services because of their view that, due to his/her present status and decline, the patient will not substantially benefit from clinical services.

SECTION 9: CRITICAL THINKING IN CLINICAL SERVICE DELIVERY: THE INTERVENTION PROCESS PROMPTS

This section includes the task prompts that we have created that are related to the SLP intervention process. We have divided the prompts into those related to three populations, pediatric, adult, and geriatric. Within each of these populations, we have then divided the prompts into those that represent potential clinical conditions presented by patients and those that reflect issues that may arise in the course of clinical service delivery. For each population, we have created 75 clinical conditions–related prompts and 25 clinical issues–related prompts, for a total of 300 prompts across the task in which you can evaluate your own critical thinking or the skills of one for whom you are a mentor.

When, in our own clinical practice, we provide SLP intervention services for patients, we receive diagnoses of their conditions either from the patients, their family members, or the professionals who have referred them to us. We also receive information about their characteristics from various kinds of documentation they forward to us: patient history forms, previous evaluation and treatment records, and referral sheets. Descriptions of the concerns we may address in the intervention process can be as extensive as an entire case file or as abbreviated as capsule statements. Because of the diversity in this information, we faced a decision as to how to construct the prompts to which students and practitioners will respond in order for the evaluation of their own level of critical thinking to commence. We considered whether we should provide detailed diagnoses and evaluation reports but ultimately decided that we would provide capsule statements. While less open-ended than a statement such as, "Please plan a course of intervention for a patient," capsule statements, with their minimal detail that but hints at the specific traits of the patient, allow the respondents to the task the most latitude in how they describe their approach to intervention that will allow them to reach their desired clinical outcomes. The prompts that follow, while not verbatim, are representative of the statements that we have received in response to the questions, "What are the clinical priorities for this SLP intervention?" and "What is the nature of the concern that is the basis for this SLP intervention?"

PEDIATRIC

Clinical Conditions

Please Note: These statements represent capsule diagnostic statements from SLP evaluation reports.

Prompt 1. "The patient presents delayed language development. While comprehension of language appears within normal limits, expression is restricted to non-language vocalizations in the absence of conventional language."

Prompt 2. "The patient presents delayed language development characterized by a typical sequence of development, as noted in the language skills he/she has attained to this point, but an atypical rate of development."

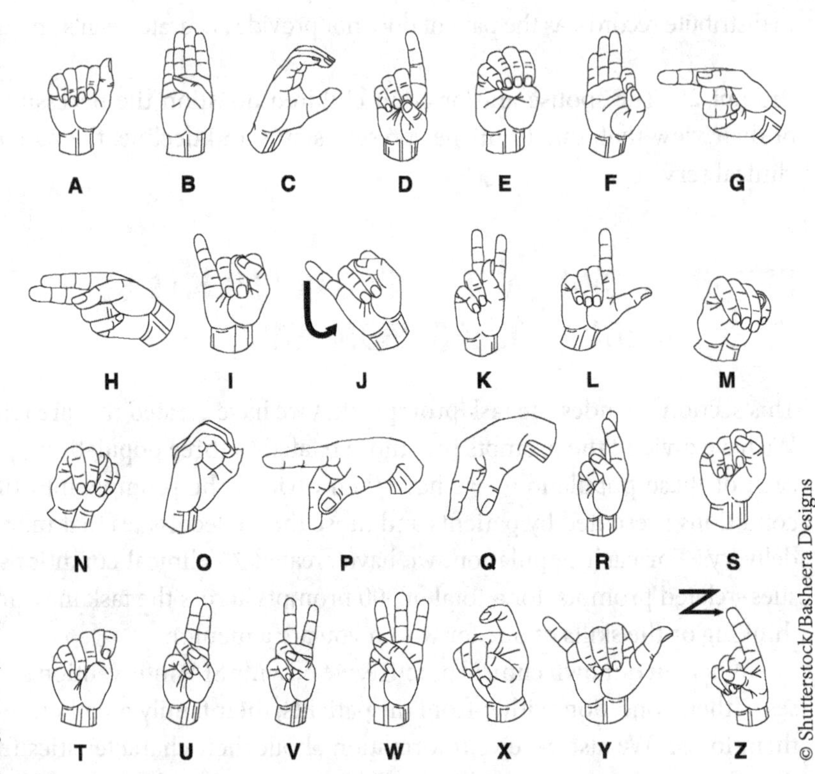

Prompt 3. "The patient presents language comprehension within normal limits but language production characterized by primarily one- and two-word utterances, with minimal simple and no compound/complex syntax."

Prompt 4. "The student presents with a language disorder centered in the semantic domain and characterized by confusion and frequent substitutions of semantically related words when he/she inserts them into utterances."

Prompt 5. "The student presents with difficulty in word recall in tasks that involve confrontational naming, as well as in tasks that involve organizing and presenting information in both oral and written form, such as in reports."

Prompt 6. "The student presents with a language disorder characterized by the inability to easily relate information from multiple sources to a theme, as well as the inability to express information clearly and correctly."

Prompt 7. "The child presents with a speech sound production condition characterized by the deletion of word final phonemes and word final syllables. The presence of these deletions results in homonymy in his/her speech."

Prompt 8. "The child presents with a delay in language development characterized by the persistence of continued production of morphophonemic patterns more characteristic of earlier points in morpheme development."

Prompt 9. "The child presents with a semantic-syntactic language disorder characterized by confusion in semantic content and transpositions within word order, both of which lead to reductions in language complexity."

Prompt 10. "The student presents with a written language disorder, specifically in the construction of narrative structures, which are characterized by a variety of applications of incorrect syntactic rules in their microstructure."

Prompt 11. "The student presents with the deficiencies in his/her comprehension and production of narrative structures, specifically narratives that contain step-by-step instructions on how to complete a variety of procedures."

Prompt 12. "The student presents with a language disorder characterized by difficulties in the production of narrative structures, specifically stories, which have no easily discernable macrostructure, either topical or temporal."

Prompt 13. "The patient presents with a semantic-pragmatic language disorder characterized by severe deficits in nonlinguistic behaviors and severe deficits in both comprehension and production of semantic content."

Prompt 14. "The patient presents with a language disorder characterized by communication apprehension, as seen in avoidance of interactions across potential communication partners and potential communication contexts."

Prompt 15. "The patient presents with a language disorder characterized by immediate non-communicative non-mitigated echolalia, accompanied by self-injurious behaviors and apparent non-comprehension of language."

Prompt 16. "The student presents with a written language disorder, as evidenced by the inability to read age- and grade-appropriate words by sound and the ability to read but not comprehend one-syllable words by sight."

Prompt 17. "The student presents with difficulties with metalinguistic skills related to phonology, specifically building up and breaking down words, building up and breaking down syllables, and creating rhyming word pairs."

Prompt 18. "The student presents with a semantic-pragmatic language disorder characterized by difficulties in the interpretation of non-literal language forms and the interpretation of the social norms applied across situations."

Prompt 19. "The patient presented with selective mutism characterized by his/her refusal to use oral communication with other people, as well as by his/her refusal to communicate in locations other than the bedroom."

Prompt 20. "The patient presented with a severe speech production disorder characterized by unintelligible speech, with no more than 25% of utterances understood by family members familiar with the speech patterns he/she produces."

Prompt 21. "The patient presented with misarticulation of multisyllable, phonetically complex words. The structural composition of these words was such that a patient in this period should have correctly produced them."

Prompt 22. "The child presented with multiple errors in phoneme production. The errors affected both vowels and consonants. Neither the vowels nor the consonants produced in error were phonetically or phonemically related."

Prompt 23. "The child presented with phoneme production errors that included distortions of and substitutions for consonants in both the fricative and affricate classes with both lingua-dental and lingua-palatal placements."

Prompt 24. "The child presented with an articulation disorder secondary to a craniofacial anomaly (specifically, complete bilateral cleft) that affected all phoneme classes and was accompanied by compensatory behaviors."

Prompt 25. "The child presented with suspected CAS characterized by inconsistent error patterns (which included phoneme deletions and phoneme reversals that compromised word shapes and reduced intelligibility)."

Prompt 26. "The child presented with a chronic pattern of word mispronunciation. While articulation of phonemes was within normal limits for his/her development level, his/her patterns of syllable stress were disrupted."

Prompt 27. "The child presented with a speech sound-production disorder characterized by the inability to reproduce a variety of speech models imitatively, accompanied by a suspected speech sound-perception disorder."

Prompt 28. "The child presented with multiple speech sound-production errors that appeared habitual, as evidence ruled out the conditions of articulation disorder, phonological disorder, and motor speech disorders."

Prompt 29. "The child presented with fossilized speech sound-production errors, characterized by the inability to produce the phonemes correctly in response to physical manipulation, auditory stimulation, and other methods."

Prompt 30. "The child presented with a speech disorder characterized by the insertion of non-speech productions into the speech. The cause and the prognosis for improvement of the condition were undetermined."

Prompt 31. "The child presented with apparent CAS, with patterns of phoneme deletions, phoneme reversals, and phoneme substitutions, as well as multiple incorrect productions per word and minimal speech imitation skill."

Prompt 32. "The child presented with a severe speech disorder characterized by the reduction of the structure of words to either C or V structure, which resulted in minimal speech intelligibility for familiar listeners and topics."

Prompt 33. "The child presented with a mild to moderate speech disorder, with the secondary characteristics of communication apprehension as seen in decreased speech output in the presence of peers and in the classroom."

Prompt 34. "The patient presented with spastic dysarthria secondary to cerebral palsy and characterized by inconsistent vocal loudness, weak pressure consonants, vocal harshness and strain, and hypernasal voice quality."

Prompt 35. "The patient presented with ataxic dysarthria secondary to anoxia and characterized by uncoordinated movements, slow speech rate, imprecise speech articulation, and disrupted speech stress pattern."

Prompt 36. "The patient presented with chronic drool secondary to dysarthria, as well as several speech and voice characteristics of the dysarthria: minimal pitch variation, minimal loudness variation, and nasal emissions."

Prompt 37. "The patient presented with a severe articulation disorder secondary to a complete (type 4) bilateral cleft within the oral-facial structures and accompanied by malocclusion and multiple dental conditions."

Prompt 38. "The patient presented with oral dysphagia characterized by weak suck and swallow patterns, as well as a voice disorder characterized by velopharyngeal incompetence secondary to a submucous palatal cleft."

Prompt 39. "The patient presented with an oromyofunctional disorder characterized by an open mouth position and an anterior lingual resting position and accompanied by a mild speech sound distortion for multiple phonemes."

Prompt 40. "The patient presents with a communication disorder characterized by the use of increased vocal loudness across communication situations. At this time, the specific cause of the condition remains undetermined."

Prompt 41. "The patient presents with a communication disorder characterized by the use of decreased vocal loudness across communication situations. At this time, the specific cause of the condition remains undetermined."

Prompt 42. "The patient presents with a communication disorder characterized by the use of both imitatively produced and non-imitatively produced non-speech noises that are potentially abusive to the speech mechanism."

Prompt 43. "The student presents with a voice disorder characterized by chronic hoarseness and diminished loudness over the course of the day, accompanied by frequent vocal abuse, such as coughing and throat clearing."

Prompt 44. "The student presents with a voice disorder characterized by denasal resonance. At this time, the patient history is negative for seasonal allergies or any respiratory infections typically characterized by denasality."

Prompt 45. "The student presents with a pattern of voice production characterized by intermittent atypical vocal resonance consistent with the condition of hypernasality, which is accompanied by intermittent nasal emission."

Prompt 46. "The child presents with dysfluency characterized by part-word and whole-word repetitions and prolongations that fluctuated across situations and were most common in attempted complex sentence productions."

Prompt 47. "The child presents with a fluency disorder characterized by primary characteristics of part-word and whole-word repetitions and whole-word interjections and secondary characteristic of decreased eye contact."

Prompt 48. "The child presents with severe communication apprehension characterized by frequent avoidance of situations, such as oral presentations to his/her classmates and phone calls with familiar and unfamiliar persons."

Prompt 49. "The student presents with a speech rate that is inappropriately fast. The child self-monitors and self-corrects for short periods of time before reversion. The cause of this conditions remains uncertain at this time."

Prompt 50. "The student presents with a speech rate that is inappropriately slow. The cause of this condition remains uncertain at this time. Neither language processing nor language production disorder has been ruled out."

Prompt 51. "The student presents with a communication disorder characterized by the inability to produce the appropriate syllable stress patterns for unfamiliar and/or structurally complex words (such as multisyllabic words)."

Prompt 52. "The child presented with a speech and language disorder secondary to concussion and characterized by confusion in the comprehension and production of information and distorted speech production."

Prompt 53. "The child presented with fluctuations in language comprehension and production, accompanied by altered affect and mood, secondary to moderate traumatic brain injury experienced in a motor vehicle accident."

Prompt 54. "The child presented with moderate deficits in comprehension and production of academic language, accompanied by decreased attention to sensory input, secondary to his/her history of petit mal seizures."

Prompt 55. "The patient presents with speech and language disorder secondary to a history of grand mal seizures and characterized by substantial deficits related to retention, retrieval, and reproduction of information."

Prompt 56. "The patient presents with deficits in speech production secondary to a severe idiopathic headache and characterized by mild unilateral paresis of the speech production musculature and imprecision in articulation."

Prompt 57. "The patient presents with intermittent episodes of difficulties with language comprehension and language formulation secondary to a suspected concussion experienced in the course of a recent football tackle."

Prompt 58. "The patient presents as 'at-risk' for delayed speech and language development secondary to a suspected severe to profound hearing loss, as indicated in a recent failure of a newborn infant hearing screening."

Prompt 59. "The patient presents with a severe speech disorder secondary to severe bilateral sensorineural hearing loss and characterized by reduced auditory comprehension and compromised speech production accuracy."

Prompt 60. "The patient presents with delayed language development, secondary to otitis media and characterized by the persistence of simplified language structure past the point of developmental appropriateness."

Prompt 61. "The child presented with severely diminished auditory comprehension of language characterized by non-responsiveness to auditory presentations of language and secondary to a suspected processing disorder."

Prompt 62. "The child, who is a candidate for an alternative or augmentative communication system, presented with speech and language disorder accompanied by a history of minimal improvement after intensive intervention."

Prompt 63. "The child, who presents with a severe speech and language disorder, is a potential candidate for an alternative and/or augmentative communication system, which could be either unaided or aided based on status."

Prompt 64. "The child, presently a high-tech augmentative communication system user, should participate in a period of diagnostic therapy to determine whether he/she could benefit from adjustments to this specific system."

Prompt 65. "The child, presently a user of both manual and oral communication, should participate in a period of diagnostic therapy to determine whether the use of one or a combination of modalities is his/her better option."

Prompt 66. "The child presents with mutism, which may be indicative of the pattern of 'silent period' that is characteristic of children in the process of bilingual development or which may be indicative of selective mutism."

Prompt 67. "The child, who is in the process of bilingual development, presents with stronger language comprehension and production in L1 than in L2, which may indicate the dominance of the language rules of L1."

Prompt 68. "The child has the potential for multilingual language development and should participate in a period of observation/parent consultation to determine the most appropriate course for introduction of languages."

Prompt 69. "The child presents with a communication difference characterized by the production of a regional dialect and accompanied by non-positive reactions from varied communication partners that should be addressed."

Prompt 70. "The student presented with a written language disorder characterized by poor manual formulation of both print and cursive letters and subsequent illegible work, accompanied by mixed dominance for handedness."

Prompt 71. "The student presented with a written language disorder characterized by weaknesses in the production of both an appropriate macrostructure and an intact microstructure within his/her written narratives."

Prompt 72. "The student presented with a written language disorder characterized by difficulties in the comprehension and interpretation of written narratives when asked to paraphrase or answer questions about them."

Prompt 73. "The patient presented with failure to thrive secondary to oral dysphagia characterized by food preferences, refusals of selected foods based on texture and color, and frequent expectoration of undesired foods."

Prompt 74. "The patient presented with oral, pharyngeal, and esophageal dysphagia characterized by penetration and aspiration of both liquids and solids and accompanied by regurgitation and excessive secretions."

Prompt 75. "The patient presented with failure to thrive secondary to severe oral, pharyngeal, and esophageal dysphagia. The patient should thus be further evaluated as a candidate for an alternate nutritional delivery system."

PEDIATRIC

Clinical Issues

Prompt 1. The parents of the child have unusual explanations for the causes of communication disorders, which resemble folklore (for instance, the idea that nutritional patterns or specific vaccines cause such disorders).

Prompt 2. The parents of the child insist that the SLP provide a clear, comprehensive explanation for the cause of the communication disorder their child presents so that the cause can inform the course of treatment.

Prompt 3. Prior to the time of the appointment, the parents of the child request that you include specific procedures in the treatment process, such as specific methods or specific materials that they have come to support.

Prompt 4. The parents indicate that their desire in intervention is that you, the SLP, treat a specific diagnosis of a communication disorder – even if not appropriate – for one or more reasons that they consider very important.

Prompt 5. The parents of the child, even after explanations, misinterpret the data collection process (and the nature of the data) that you have established to track the performance of their child across the treatment sessions.

Prompt 6. The parents of the child, even after explanations, do not understand the differences across similar conditions or disorders and thus use inappropriate labels for the pattern of communication in need of treatment.

Prompt 7. The parents of the child are unclear as to why specific clinical tools are included in the treatment of their child in terms of the purpose, procedures, potential results, and pros/cons for specific clinical tools/tasks.

Prompt 8. The parents of the child, even after explanations, are unclear as to the nature of a specific intervention for a communication disorder and how that intervention relates to the evaluation results of the child.

Prompt 9. The parents of the child have received a recommended treatment from another SLP. They disagree with that particular treatment and have consulted with you to obtain a second opinion related to the intervention.

Prompt 10. The parents of the child have received a recommended treatment. After a consultation with them, you discover that you disagree with the recommendation and must present the rationale for your view to the parents.

Prompt 11. The parents of the child have received multiple recommendations for treatment for the communication disorder their child presents. They have become confused about the reason(s) for such variation.

Prompt 12. You, the SLP, provide the parents with recommended treatment based on the diagnosis for their child. The parents disagree with your recommendation because they also do not agree with your original diagnosis.

Prompt 13. After you present your recommendations to the parents of a child, they disagree with each other as to whether to comply with this course of treatment, and each parent pressures you, the SLP, to affirm/alter your view.

Prompt 14. You believe that information from consultations with other professionals would be helpful in the treatment process. However, the parents of the child have not complied with your request that they pursue these.

Prompt 15. You believe that information from prior documentation of clinical services (evaluation and treatment) from other professionals would be helpful, but the parents refuse permission for you to receive this.

Prompt 16. After your intervention, the parents of the child insist that your report include specific information related to your descriptions of the performance of the child and your provision of the numerical intervention results.

Prompt 17. After your intervention, the parents of the child insist that your report include specific recommendations that will increase the likelihood that the child will/will not receive certain professional services.

Prompt 18. After your intervention, you present what you consider appropriate recommendations (such as for reevaluation or continuation). However, the parents of the child do not intend to comply with recommendations.

Prompt 19. The parents of the child report that they consider information from internet-based sources reliable and that they frequently visit a variety of websites to acquire information about appropriate intervention methods.

Prompt 20. The parents of the child name several television shows they watch and several television personalities they trust, particularly with respect to information related to how to address various clinical conditions.

Prompt 21. In the course of the treatment, the child does not consistently demonstrate compliance with the clinical procedures as seen in his/her responses to your requests for his/her attention or performance of behaviors.

Prompt 22. Because you believe that the evaluation results overestimate the actual level of communication skill presented by the child, you question which skills and which skill levels to start to address in the intervention process.

Prompt 23. Because you believe that the evaluation results underestimate the actual level of communication skill presented by the child, you question which skills and which skill levels to address in the intervention process.

Prompt 24. In the course of your interaction with the family, because of an implicit or explicit communication or because of attitudes or actions, you become concerned that a parent(s) poses a serious threat to your welfare.

Prompt 25. In the course of your interaction with the family, you become concerned that the information literacy level of the parents is such that they cannot effectively participate in the intervention process for their child.

ADULT

Clinical Conditions

Please Note: These statements represent capsule diagnostic statements from SLP evaluation reports.

Prompt 1. "The client presents with a communication disorder secondary to a developmental delay and could benefit from intervention directed toward the comprehension and production of language related to vocational skills."

Prompt 2. "The client presents with a communication disorder secondary to a developmental delay and that primarily affects conversational and interactional skills, specifically the mastery of frequently used social routines."

Prompt 3. "The client presents with a language disorder that affects language comprehension, specifically related to the differentiation of the content of and appropriate selection of semantically related vocabulary items."

Prompt 4. "The employee presents with a language disorder specifically related to the pragmatic language dimension, as seen in his/her audience analysis with respect to the appropriate level of language content to use."

Prompt 5. "The employee presents with a language comprehension and production disorder characterized by deficits in his/her identification of themes in and preparation of summaries of information contained in materials."

Prompt 6. "The employee presents with a communication disorder that affects the semantic dimension of his/her language and that specifically affects his/her ability to self-monitor and self-correct information produced."

Prompt 7. "The client presents with an articulation disorder characterized by fossilized errors that affect a sound class across word-initial, word-medial, and word-final positions and that are resistant to efforts at correction."

Prompt 8. "The client presents with a speech production disorder characterized by the misarticulation and mispronunciation of words, accompanied by decreased auditory discrimination of phonetically similar productions."

Prompt 9. "The client presents with a language production disorder specifically in the structural dimension of morphology and characterized by the overgeneralization of rules for bound morpheme additions to root words."

Prompt 10. "The patient presents with a mild language disorder in the area of language structure characterized by the inability to correctly discern the appropriate bound morphemes to use for contrastive and other meanings."

Prompt 11. "The patient presents with a mild language disorder that affects both language content and language structure, specifically his/her ability to match the most effective structure for the content to be expressed."

Prompt 12. "The patient presents with a language production disorder characterized by difficulty with the formulation of the macrostructure – either topical or temporal – of narratives, specifically instructions or directions."

Prompt 13. "The employee presents a moderate communication disorder characterized by deficits in his/her interpersonal communication skills, particularly those related to professional discussions, presentations, and tasks."

Prompt 14. "The employee presents communication differences that have the potential to substantially diminish professional communication effectiveness, such difficulties with professional communication expectations."

Prompt 15. "The employee presents with a communication disorder characterized by multiple forms of vocal abuse that increase his/her risk of development of a voice disorder and that are a distraction to other employees."

Prompt 16. "The patient presented with the potential for development of a communication disorder characterized by vocal abuse and misuse, specifically frequent exposure to air pollutants and minimal fluid intake."

Prompt 17. "The patient presented with a moderate voice disorder characterized by chronic laryngitis (in the absence of either vocal abuse or misuse) that resulted in vocal qualities of breathiness, hoarseness, and harshness."

Prompt 18. "The patient presented with a voice disorder characterized by disruption in healthy vocal quality (such as vocal fry and vocal harshness) and decreased healthy vocal quality as a consequence of increased vocal use."

Prompt 19. "The client presented with a voice disorder characterized by a decline in fundamental frequency over time, as well as a decrease in vocal intensity over time to the point of intermittent vocal inaudibility to listeners."

Prompt 20. "The client presented with a voice disorder characterized by the inability to sustain the airflow for voice production purposes even in the absence of exertion and even with conscious effort to control the airflow."

Prompt 21. "The client presented with a voice disorder characterized by hyponasality, which has resulted in decreased communication effectiveness and a pattern that has been a mild distraction to communication partners."

Prompt 22. "The client presented with a communication disorder with characteristics consistent with a mild hypernasality of voice or a mild nasal assimilation in articulation of phonemes, with evidence to support each option."

Prompt 23. "The patient presented with a voice disorder characterized by a pattern of vocal pitch inconsistent with his/her status as an adult and frequently misinterpreted by listeners who are unfamiliar with his/her pattern."

Prompt 24. "The patient presented with a voice disorder characterized by a pattern of vocal pitch inconsistent with his/her status as a male/female and frequently misinterpreted by listeners who are unfamiliar with the patient."

Prompt 25. "The employee presents with a voice disorder characterized by a pattern of vocal intensity that is inappropriately loud across a variety of professional situations and that serves as a distraction for other employees."

Prompt 26. "The employee presents with a voice disorder characterized by a pattern of vocal intensity that is inappropriately soft across a variety of professional situations and that serves as a distraction for other employees."

Prompt 27. "The employee presents with a voice disorder characterized by a pattern of pitch breaks of sufficient frequency that they have become a distraction to coworkers and a source of interference with office communication."

Prompt 28. "The patient presents with a voice disorder characterized by a pattern of loudness breaks of sufficient frequency that they have become a distraction to friends and a source of interference with communication."

Prompt 29. "The patient presents with a previously treated articulation disorder characterized by the persistence of the inability to produce a specific phoneme across word positions and levels of phonetic complexity."

Prompt 30. "The patient presents with a speech production disorder characterized by multiple misarticulations and mispronunciations of words, accompanied with notable self-consciousness about this on the part of the patient."

Prompt 31. "The patient presents with a communication disorder characterized by the mispronunciations of both phonetically simple and phonetically complex words and the need for multiple attempts to achieve accuracy."

Prompt 32. "The patient presents with a communication disorder characterized by the inability to easily pronounce technical words. Mastery of the production of these words is essential for his/her professional success."

Prompt 33. "The patient presents with an oromyofunctional disorder, which has the potential to compromise the articulation of lingual phonemes because of the anterior lingual position and the current status of the dentition."

Prompt 34. "The patient presents with an oromyofunctional disorder and increased risk for a disorder of articulation of phonemes, accompanied by oral drooling and oral leaking secondary to mild bilateral facial paresis."

Prompt 35. "The patient presents with dysarthria, accompanied by bilateral facial paresis, incomplete labial closure, and partial lingual protrusion and elevation, and characterized by notably decreased speech intelligibility."

Prompt 36. "The patient presents with dysarthria, characterized by substantially decreased speech rate, hyponasal vocal quality, difficulty with speech initiation, and exaggerated compensatory mandibular movements."

Prompt 37. "The patient presented with the persistence of patterns of simplifications of word productions (such as reversing, deleting, and substituting phonemes) even after extensive therapy in both childhood and adulthood."

Prompt 38. "The patient presented with apraxia of speech, secondary to CVA and characterized by uncoordinated and inconsistent movements, increased speech sound deletion, and decreased speech intelligibility."

Prompt 39. "The patient presented with a fluency disorder (specifically, stuttering) characterized by the primary symptoms of phoneme repetitions, prolongations, and interjections and by secondary physical symptoms."

Prompt 40. "The patient presented with developmental stuttering, for which he/she participated in direct therapy as a child and indirect therapy as an adult and for which he/she now wanted to pursue additional treatment."

Prompt 41. "The patient presented with a severe fluency disorder characterized by the presence of primary speech behaviors accompanied by multiple secondary physical behaviors that he/she wanted to learn to control."

Prompt 42. "The patient presents with communication apprehension in an assortment of personal and professional communication situations and desires to address his/her emotions and avoidance in the intervention."

Prompt 43. "The patient presents with a fluency disorder characterized by an excessively fast rate of speech. This rate is a distraction to listeners, who frequently ask the patient to adjust his/her speech rate (without success)."

Prompt 44. "The patient presents with a fluency disorder characterized by an excessively slow rate of speech. This rate is a distraction to listeners, who frequently ask the patient to adjust his/her speech rate (without success)."

Prompt 45. "The patient presents with a communication disorder characterized by inappropriate patterns of syllable stress for multisyllabic words, which results in disruption of the pattern of rhythm within connected speech."

Prompt 46. "The employee presents with a communication disorder characterized by extreme fluctuations in speech rate, very fast to very slow, which results in disruption of the pattern of rhythm within connected speech."

Prompt 47. "The employee presents with communication apprehension, which has resulted in avoidance of professional communication situations and diminished self-confidence with respect to oral presentation abilities."

Prompt 48. "The employee presents with a communication disorder characterized by deficits in interactional, conversational, and presentational skills that have severely compromised his/her completion of work-related duties."

Prompt 49. "Secondary to post-lingual deafness (secondary to reaction to chemotherapy), the patient presented with compromised oral communication and would benefit from treatment enhancing speechreading and speaking."

Prompt 50. "Secondary to pre-lingual deafness (secondary to anoxia at birth), the patient presented with competence across communication modalities and should be considered as a potential cochlear implant candidate."

Prompt 51. "The patient presented speech reception, discrimination, and production difficulties consistent with a noise-induced bilateral sensorineural hearing loss, as well as increased risk for voice disorder due to vocal abuse."

Prompt 52. "The patient presented with diminished speech reception and speech discrimination secondary to presbycusis and would be a candidate for hearing conservation, speech reading, and other rehabilitation services."

Prompt 53. "The patient presented with oral and pharyngeal dysphagia secondary to suspected MS and accompanied by extended idiopathic pauses reflected in issues with his/her language formulation and/or production."

Prompt 54. "The patient presented with oral and pharyngeal dysphagia secondary to early-onset Parkinson's disease and complicated by muscle weakness, difficulties with sitting, walking, self-feeding, and communicating."

Prompt 55. "The client, who uses a high-tech augmentative communication system, should participate in a course of diagnostic therapy to determine whether his/her current system is most appropriate for his/her needs."

Prompt 56. "The client, who has expressive aphasia and motor speech disorder secondary to a CVA, could benefit from an augmentative or alternative communication system but is adamant in his/her refusal to use such."

Prompt 57. "The client, who has aphasia secondary to a CVA, presently demonstrates a rate of improvement consistent with the attainment of a plateau. He/she should continue in treatment with updated therapy priorities."

Prompt 58. "The patient presented with regression in his/her regained language skills post-aphasia secondary to a CVA. He/she would benefit from the resumption of treatment, as well as from appropriate supportive services."

Prompt 59. "The patient presented with expressive aphasia characterized by both semantic and phonetic paraphasic productions and complicated by frustration related to the status of his/her expressive communication."

Prompt 60. "The patient presented with severe deficits in language comprehension secondary to a CVA and characterized by only minimal comprehension of information presented across oral, written, and manual modalities."

Prompt 61. "The patient presented with memory deficits (and associated conversational and interactional difficulties) secondary to the onset of primary progressive aphasia. Treatment should focus on memory strategies."

Prompt 62. "The patient presented with diminished communication competency in both comprehension and expression, accompanied by combative violent behaviors and secondary to a suspected primary progressive aphasia."

Prompt 63. "The patient presented with transient communication difficulties, primarily in language expression and secondary to an acquired brain injury, which should be addressed in treatment to stabilize his/her competence."

Prompt 64. "The patient presented with a severe communication disorder secondary to a MVA one year prior and characterized by the need for augmentative communication systems (presently low-tech aided and unaided)."

Prompt 65. "The patient presented with a severe communication disorder and suspected emotional trauma secondary to an assault and characterized by withdrawal from communication except in infrequent circumstances."

Prompt 66. "The patient presented with cognitive deficits associated with an acquired brain injury that affected multiple executive functions (and communication skills associated with them) and accompanied by anosognosia."

Prompt 67. "The patient presented with post-laryngectomy aphonia and a history of difficulty with the production of esophageal speech, with esophageal speech production presently characterized by breathy quality."

Prompt 68. "The patient presented with preoperative concerns about post-laryngectomy options for communication (particularly immediately after his/her procedures) and would benefit from informational support."

Prompt 69. "The patient, who used a speech valve, presented concerns about the valve characterized by a belief that he/she could improve on communication. A period of diagnostic therapy is recommended."

Prompt 70. "The patient presented with oral and pharyngeal dysphagia secondary to tracheostomy. A period of treatment to address issues related to dysphagia, accompanied by a series of speech valve trials, is recommended."

Prompt 71. "The patient presented with severe oral and pharyngeal dysphagia characterized by both penetration and aspiration of liquids and solids and accompanied by weak clearance of the bolus from the oral cavity."

Prompt 72. "The patient presented with oral dysphagia characterized by insufficient labial seal that led to oral leakage, as well as inappropriately sized sips and bites. A course of treatment to address the difficulties is advised."

Prompt 73. "The client presented with oral and pharyngeal dysphagia characterized by difficulty with his/her intake of multiple solid and liquid textures and thicknesses, as well as atypical pharyngeal sensations after intake."

Prompt 74. "The client presented with a communication difference in the form of accented English, his/her second language, that resulted in decreased speech intelligibility that should be addressed in accent modification."

Prompt 75. "The client presented with a communication difference in the form of a regional American English accent that decreased his/her self-confidence in communication and should be addressed in accent modification."

ADULT

Clinical Issues

Prompt 1. The patient repeatedly questions the cause of the communication disorder you have treated and asks you to explore every aspect of his/her personal and medical history to specifically identify one or more causes.

Prompt 2. The patient asks whether some of his/her own behaviors have contributed to the presence of the communication disorder and may or may not accept responsibility for his/her role related to the disorder.

Prompt 3. Prior to treatment appointments, the patient requests that you perform specific procedures, which may or may not be relevant to your intervention methods, because of his/her belief that these are valuable.

Prompt 4. At the start of treatment appointments, the patient indicates a desire for a specific diagnosis for a personal reason (such as to participate in a specific course of treatment that he/she believes is a desirable approach).

Prompt 5. The patient appears unclear as to the purpose of some of the treatment tasks and questions what information such tasks contribute to the treatment process, even after clear explanations from the SLP about them.

Prompt 6. The patient misinterprets data from the treatment documentation data collected in the course of the sessions and, because of this, reaches inaccurate conclusions about the current status of his/her communication.

Prompt 7. Because of his/her literacy level, the patient does not comprehend the treatment reports prepared by the SLP, and he/she thus files the report and does not ask the SLP to assist him/her to understand the contents.

Prompt 8. The patient reacts to certain aspects of the content of the treatment report with requests to the SLP to remove or, as a minimum, rephrase this information for reasons such as denial, discomfort, or disappointment.

Prompt 9. The patient provides inaccurate information about his/her home-based treatment, which leads to underestimation and/or overestimation of his/her current level and inappropriate intervention recommendations.

Prompt 10. The patient provides inaccurate history information, intentionally, which leads to underestimation and/or overestimation of his/her current level of skill thus inappropriate recommendations in the treatment plan.

Prompt 11. In response to your request that the patient set appointments with other service providers, the patient does not comply with your perception that information from them is important to the treatment process.

Prompt 12. In response to your presentation of recommendations based upon the treatment results and conclusions, the patient does not comply with these recommendations for reasons that he/she does not disclose.

Prompt 13. The patient disagrees with your diagnosis of a communication disorder and, in response to your diagnosis and treatment recommendations, argues with your interpretations information related to the condition.

Prompt 14. The patient disagrees with specific recommendations that you made at the commencement of treatment and requests that you replace these recommendations with others that are more desirable to him/her.

Prompt 15. Because of what you observed in the course of the treatment, you believe that the results of various standardized evaluation procedures presented an overestimation of the level of communication skill of the patient.

Prompt 16. Because of what you observed in the course of the treatment, you believe that the results of various standardized evaluation procedures presented an underestimation of the level of communication skill of the patient.

Prompt 17. The patient knows (either personally or professionally) other patients whom you serve. In the course of the treatment, he/she solicits information from you about the services you have provided to these people.

Prompt 18. At the conclusion of the treatment, the patient refuses permission for you to forward a duplicate of the treatment report to his/her referral source and indicates that he/she will not verbally share treatment results.

Prompt 19. Based on the behavior of the patient in the course of the treatment, you as the SLP conclude that you would be prudent to request a threat assessment to determine whether the patient could compromise your safety.

Prompt 20. While in treatment, the patient frequently contacts you, the SLP, by email and voice mail at both your office and your home, with increased references to personal information that you did not disclose to the patient.

Prompt 21. While the patient seriously considers your treatment recommendations, he/she indicates that the opinions of other individuals whom he/she knows professionally are more important to him/her than your opinions.

Prompt 22. While the patient seriously considers your treatment recommendations, he/she indicates that the opinions of other individuals whom he/she knows personally are more important to him/her than your opinions.

Prompt 23. You provide this treatment in response to the request from your patient for alternative services related to his/her suspected communication disorder. You agree with previous SLP treatment recommendations.

Prompt 24. You provide this treatment in response to the request from your patient for alternative services related to his/her suspected communication disorder. You disagree with previous SLP treatment recommendations.

Prompt 25. The patient presents signs that he/she is in the grieving process (such as denying, bargaining, arguing, crying, or otherwise reacting) in response to the specific treatment recommendations that you provided.

GERIATRIC

Clinical Conditions

Please Note: These statements represent capsule diagnostic statements from SLP evaluation reports.

Prompt 1. "The client presented intermittent language comprehension and language production difficulties associated with TIA. At the time of the evaluation, he/she had intact word comprehension but limited word recall."

Prompt 2. "The client presented with Broca's aphasia. He/she experienced specific difficulties with word recall, sentence construction, narrative construction, continuous speech maintenance, and abstract comprehension."

Prompt 3. The client presented with Wernicke's aphasia, a fluent aphasia, characterized by compromised language comprehension for both simple and multipart commands and severely compromised language production."

Prompt 4. "The patient presented with global aphasia that affected both language comprehension and language production across oral, written, and manual modalities. Communication was primarily imitative gestures."

Prompt 5. "The patient presented with transcortical sensory aphasia. He/she imitated monosyllable words, as well as words within commands presented to him/her, but neither comprehended commands nor named items."

Prompt 6. "The patient presented with transcortical motor aphasia. He/she understood simple commands (<3 steps), nonimitatively produced simple phrases, imitated longer phrases (>3 words), and wrote print illegibly."

Prompt 7. "The patient presents with anomia aphasia secondary to a left hemisphere CVA. The patient is unable to recall item names on command, and he/she produces correct names only in response to item descriptions."

Prompt 8. "The patient presents with conduction aphasia characterized by intact oral language comprehension but compromised (not fluent) oral language production that contains paraphasic word substitutions."

Prompt 9. "The patient presents with transcortical mixed aphasia characterized by intact language comprehension for simple motor commands but no nonimitative language production for names and descriptions."

Prompt 10. "The patient presented with crossed aphasia secondary to a right hemisphere CVA and characterized by deficits in language comprehension for following commands and language production for naming."

Prompt 11. "The patient presented with suspected subcortical aphasia, which was characterized by his/her mild deficits in language production (specifically in naming and describing various items) and a partial hemianopia."

Prompt 12. "The patient presented with acquired apraxia of speech characterized by nonimitative production of monosyllabic words imitative production of one- and two-syllable words, as well as some intact automatic speech."

Prompt 13. "The patient presented with spastic dysarthria characterized by weakness of the speech musculature, as well as by hypernasality and a harsh, strident vocal quality resulting in reduced speech intelligibility."

Prompt 14. "The patient presented with flaccid dysarthria characterized by unilateral facial paresis and incomplete labial closure, with speech attempts accompanied by drool and decreased intelligibility across listeners."

Prompt 15. "The patient presented with hypokinetic dysarthria characterized by decreased rate of speech, even for phonetically simple words, and accompanied by difficulty in the initiation of speech and exaggerated movement."

Prompt 16. "The patient presented with hyperkinetic dysarthria characterized by increased rate of speech and interjections of nonspeech noises accompanied by the vocal characteristics of strain and inconsistent phonation."

Prompt 17. "The patient presented with ataxia dysarthria characterized by distorted productions of phonemes, extended durations of vowels, decreased rate of speech, and reduced intelligibility of speech to his/her listeners."

Prompt 18. "The patient presented with memory deficiencies characterized by diminished short-term memory loss and accompanied by inappropriate language production that reflected his/her failure to remember information."

Prompt 19. "The patient presented with severe language comprehension and production difficulties secondary to Alzheimer's disease, as well as with decreased self-awareness and diminished short-term and long-term memory."

Prompt 20. "The patient presented with multi-infarct dementia characterized by interspersed periods of stability and decline, as well as by inconsistent language production that fluctuates from clear to incomprehensible."

Prompt 21. "The patient presented with Lewy body dementia, which resulted in his/her inability to perform daily self-care tasks independently and/or perform tasks to completion, as well as inappropriate language use."

Prompt 22. "The client presents with language comprehension and production difficulties secondary to mixed dementia. This includes noncompliance with desired behaviors and directions and short-term memory deficits."

Prompt 23. "The client presents with dysphagia secondary to Huntington's disease and characterized by inconsistent rate of chewing and frequent coughing related to premature oral to pharyngeal transfer of the bolus."

Prompt 24. "The client presents with dysarthria secondary to Parkinson's disease and characterized by increased speech rate, reduced speech volume, as well as the ability to self-monitor but not to sustain self-correction."

Prompt 25. "The patient presented with communication disorders secondary to primary progressive aphasia and characterized by moderate language comprehension deficiencies and severe language production deficiencies."

Prompt 26. "The patient presented with dysarthria secondary to ALS and characterized by decreased speech rate and diminished respiratory control of speech. He/she also presented with oral dysphagia with very slow chew."

Prompt 27. "The patient presented with cognitive deficits secondary to MS. These deficits, which fluctuated in severity, were characterized by memory loss and by difficulty with comprehension of concrete and abstract language."

Prompt 28. "The patient presented with cognitive deficits secondary to a MVA and characterized by the production of socially inappropriate communication and difficulty with the completion of time-sensitive activities."

Prompt 29. "The patient presented with cognitive deficits secondary to a concussion and characterized by long- and short-term memory deficits. The memory deficits appeared to have decreased for the past six months."

Prompt 30. "The patient presented with cognitive deficits (secondary to a home accident) characterized by decreased safety awareness, overestimation of skills, rationalization of errors, and the need for repeated directions."

Prompt 31. "The patient presented with cognitive deficits secondary to long-term alcohol abuse and characterized by long- and short-term memory deficits and inappropriate social communication behaviors."

Prompt 32. "The patient presented with cognitive decline secondary to long-term substance abuse and characterized by complaints of widespread pain, considerable fatigue, and the difficulty of varied cognitive tasks."

Prompt 33. "The patient presented with dysphagia characterized by his/her minimal interest in nutritional intake and denial of hunger even in the presence of favorite foods, secondary to recently diagnosed depression."

Prompt 34. "The patient presented with failure to thrive, accompanied by decreased interest in oral intake, consumption of minimal amounts of liquids and solids, substantial unintentional weight loss, and increased sleep."

Prompt 35. "The patient presented with oral dysphagla characterized by an extended duration for chewing solid food, incomplete oral clearing of solid food, and decreased sensation of residual food particles in the mouth."

Prompt 36. "The patient presented with pharyngeal dysphagia characterized by penetration of both liquids and solids into the vallecula, accompanied by frequent coughing and regurgitating followed by additional swallowing."

Prompt 37. "The patient presented with esophageal dysphagia characterized by sensations of solid food residue within the esophagus, as well as by emesis of solid foods. Oral and pharyngeal aspects of the swallow were WNL."

Prompt 38. "The patient presented with functional dysphagia characterized by difficulties with each phase of the swallow. Results of both the bedside swallow examination and the modified barium study were unremarkable."

Prompt 39. "The patient presented as post-laryngectomy (secondary to laryngeal cancer) with aphonia and, at the time of evaluation, the inability to produce esophageal speech. Communication was by mouthed words."

Prompt 40. "After a partial glossectomy, the patient presents with decreased speech intelligibility and difficulty with speech production both imitatively and non-imitatively, as well as with severe oral and pharyngeal dysphagia."

Prompt 41. "The patient, who is post-glossectomy, presents with dysphagia secondary to this procedure and should undergo oral nutrition trials. He/she also presents with reduced intelligibility and is a candidate for AAC."

Prompt 42. "The patient, who is edentulous, presents with a speech disorder characterized by multiple phoneme deletions, substitutions, distortions, and compensatory movements, with decreased speech intelligibility."

Prompt 43. "The patient, who recently had a tracheostomy, presented with a speech disorder characterized by reduced speech intelligibility, as well as with a voice disorder characterized by reduced loudness and breathy quality."

Prompt 44. "The patient, who was ventilator dependent at the time of the evaluation, presented with aphonia characterized by the inability to imitatively or non-imitatively produce vocalizations even with repeated attempts."

Prompt 45. “The patient presented with dysarthria, which resulted from his/her recent CVA. His/her speech was characterized by slow rate, frequent pauses, labial groping, tense oral and facial movements, and nasal quality.”

Prompt 46. “The patient presented with a psychogenic fluency disorder characterized by the primary dysfluency characteristic of tense pauses and the secondary dysfluency characteristic of slapping the body for initiating speech.”

Prompt 47. “The patient presented with disordered language comprehension and language production secondary to severe depression and characterized by minimal participation in interactions with family and friends.”

Prompt 48. “The patient presented with failure to thrive, as noted in recent substantial decline in physical, intellectual, and receptive/expressive communication status and accompanied by oral and pharyngeal dysphagia.”

Prompt 49. “Subsequent to a closed head injury, the patient presented with severely compromised attention, which diminished his/her ability to effectively complete and communicate appropriately for familiar daily tasks.”

Prompt 50. “The patient, who presented with anosognosia, had a communication disorder characterized by diminished interest in, attention to, and participation in communication with both familiar and unfamiliar people.”

Prompt 51. “The patient presented with anomia secondary to a CVA and accompanied by the production of phonetic and semantic paraphasias in attempts to name items on demand. Language therapy is thus recommended.”

Prompt 52. “The patient presented with circumlocution characterized by extensive descriptions (with both appropriate and inappropriate details) of physical characteristics of items and individuals without specific names.”

Prompt 53. “The patient presented with an expressive language disorder secondary to a CVA and characterized by phonetically and semantically related word substitutions. Therapy should focus on word retrieval strategies.”

Prompt 54. “The patient presented with anomia secondary to a CVA and accompanied by circumlocution and deficits in self-monitoring and self-correcting. A course of therapy to address these deficiencies appears warranted.”

Prompt 55. “The patient presented with a reading disorder as a symptom of aphasia and characterized by the inability to comprehend narratives of varied complexity levels and paraphrase and answer questions related to them.”

Prompt 56. "The patient presented with a written language disorder as a symptom of aphasia and characterized with deficits in his/her print formation, as well as word retrieval, sentence construction, and narrative construction."

Prompt 57. "The patient presented with acalculia secondary to acquired brain injury. He/she expressed concerns specifically related to mathematical calculations, such as checkbook maintenance, in the course of the day."

Prompt 58. "The patient presented with amusica, which affected his/her ability to read musical scores, as well as a voice disorder characterized by a reduced pitch range in comparison with his/her range prior to his/her CVA."

Prompt 59. "The patient presented with hemi-inattention secondary to a right hemisphere CVA, with the hemi-inattention accompanied by inappropriate language production consistent with the effects of reduced sensory input."

Prompt 60. "The patient presented with auditory hallucinations secondary to a suspected psychiatric condition, as well as a semantic/pragmatic language disorder characterized by inappropriate content for the situation at hand."

Prompt 61. "The patient presented with prosopagnosia secondary to a CVA, which affected his/her language in that he/she produced no appropriate personal names for individuals without nonvisual sensory cues provided."

Prompt 62. "The patient presented with cognitive deficits secondary to anoxia experienced in a cardiovascular event, specifically related to maintenance of attention in situations and performance of details of sequential tasks."

Prompt 63. "The patient presented with memory deficits subsequent to closed head injury and characterized by deficits in both language comprehension and language production consistent with those typical of this condition."

Prompt 64. "The patient presented with idiopathic cognitive deficits characterized by specific deficits in problem solving and reasoning and associated compromise of language comprehension and language production."

Prompt 65. "The patient presented with memory deficits subsequent to the onset of dementia and accompanied by deficits in language comprehension and production, particularly related to the formulation of narrative structure."

Prompt 66. "The patient presented with an acquired pragmatic language disorder characterized by inappropriate lexical choices and the inability to communicate effectively across interactions with other individuals."

Prompt 67. "The patient presented with a written language disorder, specifically the inability to read print above an elementary level. Therapy to establish preliteracy skills, as well as literacy instruction, would be advisable."

Prompt 68. “The patient presented with a written language disorder, specifically the ability to retrieve the lexicon and formulate the structure associated with written narratives. Both therapy and instruction are warranted.”

Prompt 69. “The patient presented with communication apprehension, characterized by his/her discomfort with public presentations. He/she would benefit from treatment in the form of communication skill enhancement.”

Prompt 70. “The patient presented with a communication difference, exemplified by his/her reticence and reluctance to participate in public discussions. He/she would benefit from services to enhance his/her effectiveness.”

Prompt 71. “The patient presented with a deficit in professional communication characterized by his/her inability to identify and comply with interactional boundaries. A course of intervention to address this is warranted.”

Prompt 72. “The employee had a language disorder that affected both comprehension and production and affected his/her ability to successfully complete detail-oriented and narrative-focused workplace tasks competently.”

Prompt 73. “The patient presented with a progressive age-related bilateral sensorineural hearing loss. He/she would benefit from aural rehabilitation services specifically focused on hearing conservation and speechreading.”

Prompt 74. “The patient, who presented with a history of Meniere’s disease, would benefit from a course of treatment focused upon speech reception and speech discrimination skills compromised by his/her severe tinnitus.”

Prompt 75. “The patient presented with difficulties in speech discrimination secondary to a hearing loss. He/she could benefit with aural rehabilitation services with a focus on phoneme, word, and phrase discrimination.”

GERIATRIC

Clinical Issues

Prompt 1. The patient does not drive in the afternoon and expresses concerns that he/she has no family members or friends who can provide transportation to and from the clinic where the SLP intervention is scheduled.

Prompt 2. The patient is confused about the specific services covered by his/her health insurance and the extent of the copayment for which he/she is responsible. He/she asks whether reduced clinical fees are available.

Prompt 3. The patient demonstrates considerable resistance to the idea of intervention. He/she continues to insist that he/she does not present a communication disorder and does not need to participate in the intervention.

Prompt 4. The patient is physically unable to participate in the intervention tasks. He/she falls asleep easily, particularly when sitting at a table. He/she also has diminished sight and hearing, with restricted motor skills.

Prompt 5. Prior to the initial intervention session, the patient or spouse requests that you perform specific procedures because the professional who referred the patient for intervention recommended these procedures.

Prompt 6. At the initial intervention session, the patient indicates a desire for a specific approach to treatment for a personal reason (such as because a friend had such treatment or such an approach is covered by insurance).

Prompt 7. The patient appears confused as to the purpose of some of the intervention tasks and how to perform them, even after clear explanations from the SLP about them and demonstrations of tasks and materials.

Prompt 8. The patient provides inaccurate information about his/her daily practice related to intervention tasks, either intentionally or unintentionally, which leads to confusion about whether the intervention is effective.

Prompt 9. In response to your request that the patient set appointments with other service providers, the patient does not or adult children do not wish to comply because they consider the appointments inconvenient.

Prompt 10. In response to your presentation of recommendations based upon the performance of the patient in intervention, the patient does not or adult children do not comply with these recommendations for unknown reasons.

Prompt 11. The patient and his/her spouse disagree with specific recommendations that you made over the course of the intervention and request that you replace these with others that are perceived as more reasonable.

Prompt 12. The patient and his/her spouse know other patients whom you serve. They question why your intervention methods and materials are so different from those you provided for them, who have similar concerns.

Prompt 13. While the patient seriously considers your approach to the intervention, he/she indicates that the opinions of other individuals whom he/she knows professionally are more important to him/her than your opinions.

Prompt 14. While the patient seriously considers your approaches to the intervention, he/she indicates that the opinions of other individuals whom he/she knows personally are more important to him/her than your opinions.

Prompt 15. Your patient has services provided by another SLP at the same time that you provide intervention. You agree with the approach (and specifically, methods and materials) implemented by this SLP for your patient.

Prompt 16. Your patient has services provided by another SLP at the same time that you provide intervention. However, you do not agree with one or more aspects of the approach implemented by this SLP for your patient.

Prompt 17. The patient presents signs that he/she is in the grieving process (such as denying, bargaining, arguing, crying, or otherwise reacting) in response to the need for intervention for his/her communication disorder.

Prompt 18. The patient and his/her spouse disagree with you about one or more aspects of the intervention approach that you have recommended that you implement. They attempt to convince you to support their position.

Prompt 19. The patient and his/her spouse disagree with each other about one or more aspects of the intervention approach that you have recommended. Each person attempts to persuade you to adopt his/her position.

Prompt 20. The patient and his/her adult children disagree with you about one or more aspects of the approach to intervention that you implement. They attempt to convince you that your approach is therefore inappropriate.

Prompt 21. The patient and family members have extensive questions about the clinical documentation associated with the intervention and contact you, the SLP, three times weekly for several weeks to overview these.

Prompt 22. The patient notes that previous SLP intervention was different from your approach. You do not agree with the approach implemented and promoted by the previous service provider, and you explain your reasons.

Prompt 23. The patient notes that previous SLP intervention was different from your approach. However, you agree with the approach implemented and promoted by the previous service provider, and you explain your reasons.

Prompt 24. Confusion exists as to who is responsible for the authorization to distribute records, as the patient does not provide accurate details about previous intervention services and does not understand informed consent.

Prompt 25. The spouse and/or adult children question the necessity for SLP intervention services because of their view that, due to his/her present status and decline, the patient will not substantially benefit from the services.

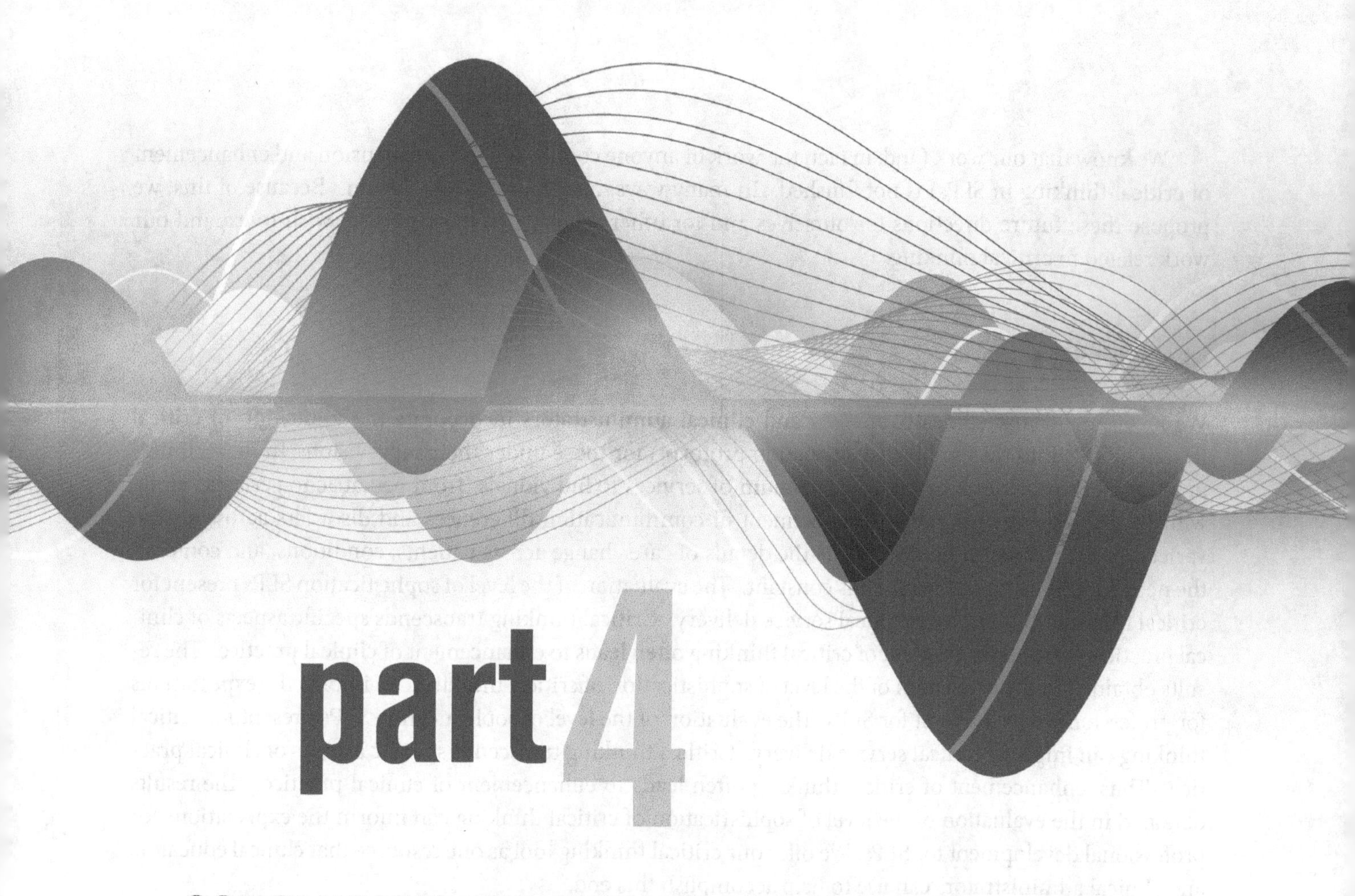

part 4

CONCLUSION AND FUTURE RECOMMENDATIONS

In this book, we have addressed critical thinking. In Section 1, we documented the value of critical thinking across personal and professional endeavors, and in Section 2, we described the themes inherent in a diverse assortment of definitions of critical thinking available from the current literature. In Section 3, we presented a model of critical thinking specific to clinical practice in SLP. Our model contains five dimensions —Information, Innovation, Interpretation, Integration, Intentionality—and four skill levels—Inexperienced, Imitative, Inquisitive, Ingenious—that both clinical students and clinical practitioners can present. To allow clinical educators and clinical administrators to ascertain the sophistication of critical thinking demonstrated by those under their supervision, we provided sets of clinical profiles and clinical issues to which clinical students and clinical practitioners can respond. The responses of participants in our task to these prompts will reveal their level of critical thinking skill for each critical thinking area we included in our model. Their patterns of performance will inform their decisions, as well as the decisions of their supervisors, about the most appropriate steps to further develop their critical thinking skills.

We know that our work (and, in fact, the work of anyone committed to the expansion and enhancement of critical thinking in SLPs) is not finished. In many ways, our work has only begun. Because of this, we propose these future directions for ourselves and for other scholar-practitioners who wish to expand our work related to critical thinking:

Recommendation 1:

We recommend that clinical educators and clinical administrators incorporate the evaluation of critical thinking skills into the established evaluation protocols for those under their supervision. In their clinical practice, SLPs provide an extended continuum of services to individuals (from pediatric to geriatric, along with their families) with a diverse assortment of communication differences and disorders across a wide variety of professional contexts. While the details of care change across patients, conditions, and contexts, the need for critical thinking remains constant. The evaluation of the level of sophistication SLPs present for critical thinking can improve clinical service delivery. Critical thinking transcends specific aspects of clinical practice. Thus, enhancement of critical thinking often leads to enhancement of clinical practice. The results obtained in the evaluation of the level of sophistication of critical thinking can inform the expectations for professional development for SLPs. The evaluation of the level of sophistication SLPs present for critical thinking can improve clinical service delivery. Critical thinking transcends specific aspects of clinical practice. Thus, enhancement of critical thinking often leads to enhancement of clinical practice. The results obtained in the evaluation of the level of sophistication of critical thinking can inform the expectations for professional development for SLPs. We offer our critical thinking tool as one resource that clinical educators and clinical administrators can use to help accomplish this end.

Recommendation 2:

We recommend that clinical educators and clinical administrators incorporate the enhancement of critical thinking skills into the established professional development plans for those under their supervision. The traditional process of clinical education has focused upon three parameters: (1) What do clinical students know? (2) How do clinical students perform very specific clinical tasks? and (3) How do clinical students apply what they know to specific clinical scenarios? This focus upon the informational and mechanical elements of practice, as well as on personal style in this context, has undoubtedly enhanced the preparation of clinical students for eventual practice. We believe, however, that the infusion of a specific focus on critical thinking into the clinical education process will elevate clinical skills to a superior level and lead to SLPs who, rather than technicians, are "thinker-practitioners" who reflect on and place each component of the clinical service delivery process into a broader framework that critical thinking provides.

Recommendation 3:

We recommend that clinical students and clinical practitioners participate in systematic self-evaluation of their own critical thinking skills. Based on our review of the literature, we appreciate that inexperienced critical thinkers may not have sufficient experience to reflect their own thinking, which may lead to their overestimation or underestimation of their own level of skill. However, we believe that, with depth and breadth of experience, they may learn to more accurately evaluate their performance across critical thinking components and, simply put, know both what they know and what they do not know. We also believe that this self-awareness is the foundation for the self-monitoring and self-correcting that enhance the critical thinking process and allow individuals to become more independent critical thinkers, more internally driven than externally driven in their development of even more advanced skills. The expectations from supervisors and administrators can foster this transition.

Recommendation 4:

We recommend that our critical thinking tool be used for purposes of data collection to advance the knowledge base related to the acquisition and/or development of critical thinking skills in SLPs across their lives, as well as to study the factors that increase or decrease the sophistication of their critical thinking across contexts. Toward this end, we have started to collect preliminary quantitative data related to the critical thinking of undergraduate students as they have analyzed the clinical services they have observed, both to establish sound inter-rater and intra-rater reliability for our tool and to document a level of performance for a population. We believe that continued research has the potential to reveal whether a developmental sequence exists for critical thinking, as well as the extent to which the nature of the task, the specificity of the instructions, the modality of the response, and other factors influence the performance of the participants in the critical thinking task. Research will allow us to continue to improve our tool.

Recommendation 5:

We recommend that the results of the evaluation of critical thinking skills with our tool inform the development of instructional methods to incorporate into pre-professional and professional contexts to enhance critical thinking in both clinical students and clinical practitioners. Toward this end, we have started to test instructional activities designed to facilitate the move of individuals from one level of skill to the next in a specific skill area within critical thinking. The creation, application, and evaluation of such activities will address such issues as whether individuals can improve their critical thinking via their participation in traditional instructional activities or, conversely, whether their improvement is an outgrowth of the more holistic internalization of critical thinking from participation in an academic and clinical curriculum over time. In either case, expansion of the pedagogical evidence base will contribute to the fulfillment of the mission to provide the best possible professional preparation for SLPs built upon a commitment to lifelong learning—which most definitely would involve (and, we hope, improve) critical thinking.

At this point, we have reached the conclusion of our book. We appreciate the time that you, our reader, have invested into your study of our ideas. We welcome opportunities for conversation with you about our shared commitment to critical thinking, as well as about your recommendations for future directions in scholarly activity in this area. Until then, we wish you continued success and satisfaction in your clinical preparation and/or clinical practice as SLPs.